P9-APW-889

Yale Studies in Political Science, 31

WILSON SCHMIDT LIBRARY
PUBLIC CHOICE CENTER

ROBERT A. DAHL

Dilemmas of Pluralist Democracy

Autonomy vs. Control

NEW HAVEN AND LONDON
YALE UNIVERSITY PRESS

Copyright © 1982 by Yale University.
All rights reserved.
This book may not be reproduced, in whole
or in part, in any form (beyond that
copying permitted by Sections 107 and 108
of the U.S. Copyright Law and except by
reviewers for the public press), without
written permission from the publishers.

Designed by James J. Johnson
and set in Caledonia Roman.
Printed in the United States of America by
Vail-Ballou Press, Binghamton, N.Y.

Library of Congress Cataloging in Publication Data

Dahl, Robert Alan, 1915–
Dilemmas of pluralist democracy.

(Yale studies in political science; 31) Includes index.
1. Democracy.   2. Pluralism (Social sciences)
3. Associations, institutions, etc.   4. Public interest.
I. Title.   II. Series.
JC423.D249   321.8   81–16111
ISBN 0–300–02543–2   AACR2

1   2   3   4   5   6   7   8   9   10

320
Dahl

TO ANN

All political societies are composed of other, smaller societies of different types, each of which has its interests and maxims. . . . The will of these particular societies always has two relations: for the members of the association, it is a general will; for the large society, it is a private will, which is very often found to be upright in the first respect and vicious in the latter.

—Rousseau, *Political Economy* (1755)

In order for the general will to be well expressed, it is therefore important that there be no partial society in the State, and that each citizen give only his own opinion. . . . If there are partial societies, their number must be multiplied and their inequality prevented. . . . These precautions are the only valid means of ensuring that the general will is always enlightened and that the people is not deceived.

—Rousseau, *On the Social Contract*, book 2, chap. 3 (1762)

The most natural privilege of man, next to the right of acting for himself, is that of combining his exertions with those of his fellow-creatures, and of acting in common with them. I am therefore led to conclude that the right of association is almost as inalienable as the right of personal liberty. No legislator can attack it without impairing the very foundations of society. Nevertheless, if the liberty of association is a fruitful source of advantages and prosperity to some nations, it may be perverted or carried to excess by others, and the element of life may be changed into an element of destruction.

—Tocqueville, *Democracy in America*, vol. 1, chap. 12 (1835)

Amongst the laws which rule human societies there is one which seems to be more precise and clear than all the others. If men are to remain civilized, or to become so, the art of associating together must grow and improve, in the same ratio in which the equality of condition is increased.

—Tocqueville, *Democracy in America*, vol. 1, second book, chap. 5 (1840)

Contents

Acknowledgments

During the time in which this brief book has been evolving out of an unfinished first draft that I circulated to colleagues eight years ago, and to which it now bears only a family resemblance, I have profited greatly from criticisms and comments offered by David Cameron, James W. Fesler, James Fishkin, Peter Hardi, Joseph LaPalombara, Charles E. Lindblom, Nelson W. Polsby, Douglas Rae, Albert Reiss, Dennis Thompson, Douglas Yates, and an anonymous reader for the Yale University Press. Several of these colleagues participated, as I did, in the weekly seminar on American Democratic Institutions held under the auspices of the Institution for Social and Policy Studies at Yale. Their contributions to the seminar have influenced my thinking and thus the way the book developed.

For their skill and patience in typing the manuscript at various stages of its evolution, I owe thanks to Rita Santorowski and Janet Wicklow. Marian Ash has, once again, performed superbly as Senior Editor at the Yale University Press; and the sensitive and sensible editing of Robert Brown has improved the text. I should also like to express my appreciation to Yale University, the John Simon Guggenheim Memorial Foundation, and the Ford Foundation for support that helped me to find time in which to read, reflect, and write.

The Underlying Dilemma

Independent organizations are highly desirable in a democracy, at least in a large-scale democracy. Whenever democratic processes are employed on a scale as large as the nation-state, autonomous organizations are bound to come into existence. They are more, however, than a direct consequence of democratizing the government of the nation-state. They are also necessary to the functioning of the democratic process itself, to minimizing government coercion, to political liberty, and to human well-being.

Yet as with individuals, so with organizations; independence or autonomy (I use the terms interchangeably) creates an opportunity to do harm. Organizations may use the opportunity to increase or perpetuate injustice rather than reduce it, to foster the narrow egoism of their members at the expense of concerns for a broader public good, and even to weaken or destroy democracy itself.

Like individuals, then, organizations ought to possess some autonomy, and at the same time they should also be controlled. Crudely stated, this is the fundamental problem of pluralist democracy. My purpose in this book is to explore the problem of pluralist democracy and some possible solutions.

The problem of pluralist democracy, or democratic pluralism (I also use these terms interchangeably), is only one aspect of a general dilemma in political life: autonomy or control? Or to ask a less simpleminded question: how much autonomy and how much control? Or to anticipate still more of the problem's complexity, how much autonomy ought to be permitted to what actors, with respect to what actions, and in relation to what other actors, including the government of the state? Plus the complementary question: how much control ought to be exercised by what actors, including the government, employing what means of control over what other actors with respect to what actions?

Posed in these general terms, the problem of democratic pluralism is very nearly a description of the entire project of political theory since its beginnings in antiquity. The aim of this book is far more limited. For one thing, as I have already indicated, my focus will be not on individuals but on organizations, a somewhat artificial but serviceable reduction in scope. The scope is narrowed further because my argument deals not with regimes of all kinds but only with democratic regimes. What is more, in a long leap over a serpent's nest of problems, I take the desirability of democracy for granted. Even so, the discussion applies not to democracies in a universal sense but only to democratic processes applied to the governments of large-scale systems—concretely, the governments of countries or nation-states.* In addition, as I do with the highly debatable question of the desirability of democracy, I make a number of assumptions that, though obviously contestable, I hope will prove acceptable enough to let me proceed with the discussion.

Finally, I make no effort to arrive at specific solutions to the problem of pluralist democracy. Specific solutions—satisfactory ones, anyway—can be arrived at only in the context of the special characteristics and predicaments of a particular country. Yet no specific solution is likely to be satisfactory unless it is informed by some guiding ideas and principles. My aim therefore is to explore certain aspects of the problem, arrive at some general conclusions about several major alternatives, and offer a few broad principles relevant to judgments about these alternative solutions.

Despite this reduced scope, the implications of the argument

---

*For many countries the term nation-state is something of a misnomer. However, in using it interchangeably with country I follow a common practice. I find the term useful in contrasting democracy on the large scale of the nation-state with democracy on the small scale of the city state.

for contemporary political ideas and ideologies extend well beyond the porous boundaries around the theory and practice of democratic pluralism. For the most powerful ideologies of our age all suffer from having acquired their shape and substance in the eighteenth and nineteenth centuries, or very much earlier, before the world in which we now live had come fully into view. They are like medieval maps of the world, charming but dangerous for navigating unfamiliar seas. In the manner of adherents to Ptolemaic cosmology after Copernicus, True Believers can maintain their traditional ideologies at the cost of adding more epicycles to the original theory; but their understanding of the world gets more and more out of joint with fresh experiences and perceptions. Liberalism, conservatism, capitalism, socialism, Marxism, corporatism, anarchism, even democratic ideas, all face a world that in its form and thrust confounds the crucial assumptions, requirements, descriptions, predictions, hopes, or prescriptions they express.

More specifically, all contemporary political theories and ideologies are menaced by the dilemma of organizational autonomy and control. Satisfactory solutions—much less ideal ones—elude both theory and practice in all technologically advanced countries, whether capitalist or socialist (to use terms that are themselves somewhat out of joint with reality). Although the dilemma is more hidden from public view in countries governed by authoritarian regimes, pressures for organizational autonomy are like coiled springs precariously restrained by the counterforce of the state and ready to unwind whenever the system is jolted.

Yet although the argument carries powerful and unsettling implications for nondemocratic regimes, what concerns me here is the problem of democratic pluralism. As we shall see, the problem is really a set of problems.

2

Clarifying the Major Premise

Independent organizations exist in all democratic countries. Consequently, the problem of democratic pluralism is a universal problem in modern democracy.

Although I believe the first sentence to be true, I doubt whether it can be shown conclusively to be true. Because it serves as a major premise for the argument of later chapters, I want now to explain what it means and why it is a reasonable assumption.

To help the reader see where this chapter is going, let me summarize the gist of it here:

As to democracy:

1. In the expressions *democratic pluralism* and *pluralist democracy*, the term *democracy* may refer either to an ideal or to a specific type of actual regime. Democracy in the ideal sense is a necessary condition for the best political order. It is not a sufficient condition.

2. Historically, the term *democracy* has been applied to two specific types of actual regimes which, though quite different from one another, have been relatively democratic by comparison with all other regimes. These are the regimes of (a) relatively democratized city-states and (b) relatively democratized nation-states (countries). The first kind of regime can be understood as an attempt to democratize small-scale governments, the second as an attempt to democratize large-scale governments. The second kind of regime may also be called polyarchy.

3. Despite certain inherent limits, nation-states (countries)

are, when judged according to the democratic ideal, the largest political units within which relatively democratized regimes will exist
in the foreseeable future. Systems smaller than countries would be
too ineffective in dealing with many crucial contemporary problems, while systems larger than countries—e.g., international organizations—are almost sure to be far less democratic than the present regimes of democratic countries.

As to pluralism:

4. In the expressions *democratic pluralism* or *pluralist democracy*, the terms *pluralism* and *pluralist* refer to organizational pluralism, that is, to the existence of a plurality of relatively autonomous (independent) organizations (subsystems) within the domain
of a state.

5. In all democratic countries, some important organizations
are relatively autonomous.

6. A country is a pluralist democracy if (a) it is a democracy
in the sense of polyarchy and (b) important organizations are relatively autonomous. Hence all democratic countries are pluralist
democracies.

Democracy as Ideal

For the better part of two thousand years, democratic processes
were typically held to apply only to very small states, like the city-
states of Greece or medieval Italy. The increasing application of
democratic ideas to nation-states from the seventeenth century onward required new political institutions radically different from
those appropriate to city-states. The new institutions both reflected
and fostered changes in ways of thinking about democracy itself. As
new forms came to be justified by older ideas, changes in political
consciousness occurred that were often subtle, elusive, and confus-
ing. Today the term *democracy* is like an ancient kitchen midden
packed with assorted leftovers from twenty-five hundred years of
nearly continuous usage.

From a number of possible ways to conceive of democracy, I

shall pick two that bear most closely on the problem of democratic pluralism. The first conceives of democracy as an ideal or theoretical system, perhaps at the extreme limit of human possibilities or even beyond. According to this interpretation, an ideal democratic process would satisfy five criteria:

1. Equality in voting: In making collective binding decisions, the expressed preference of each citizen (citizens collectively constitute the *demos*) ought to be taken equally into account in determining the final solution.

2. Effective participation: Throughout the process of collective decision making, including the stage of putting matters on the agenda, each citizen ought to have adequate and equal opportunities for expressing his or her preferences as to the final outcome.

3. Enlightened understanding: In the time permitted by the need for a decision, each citizen ought to have adequate and equal opportunities for arriving at his or her considered judgment as to the most desirable outcome.

4. Final control over the agenda: The body of citizens (the demos) should have the exclusive authority to determine what matters are or are not to be decided by means of processes that satisfy the first three criteria. (Put in another way, provided the demos does not alienate its final control over the agenda it may delegate authority to others who may make decisions by nondemocratic processes.)

5. Inclusion: The demos ought to include all adults subject to its laws, except transients.

It is hard to see how people could govern themselves if their decision-making processes failed to meet these criteria and equally difficult to understand how they could be said *not* to govern themselves if their political processes were to meet these criteria fully. Since practically all the artifacts uncovered in the kitchen midden of democracy are related to the idea of people governing themselves, it is reasonable to call a process of decision making fully democratic if and only if it meets these criteria (Dahl 1979).

The extent to which the democratic process as defined by these criteria is necessary to a good polity, or to the best, is a question I touch on only briefly in this book, since a proper examination would require a book in itself. I simply assume that the democratic process as I have just defined it is necessary to a good polity. Yet the demo-cratic process may be necessary and still not sufficient for a good polity. I assume that it is not sufficient, and in a later chapter I de-scribe a situation in which I think it would not be sufficient.

Democracy as Actual Regimes: Small Scale and Large Scale

The ideal criteria are so demanding that no actual regime has ever fully met them. Possibly none ever will. To deny the term *democracy* to any regime not fully democratic in the ideal sense would be equivalent to saying that no democratic regime has ever existed. Language so purified is inconsistent with usage in other domains of ideal value, such as justice, beauty, love, and virtue. Moreover, those who created the term *democracy* in classical Greece de-scribed certain actual regimes as democracies, as have later political theorists, philosophers, historians, and others, and ordinary lan-guage today authorizes us to do so. The kitchen midden of demo-cratic ideas furnishes several accounts of actual democratic regimes, however, each with rather different political institutions. Of these, two are particularly germane.

Historically, the first to appear were the regimes of relatively democratized city-states. Very much later came the second, the re-gimes of relatively democratized nation-states. The first exhibited some of the possibilities in popular government on a small scale, the second some of the possibilities in popular government on a large scale. Important historical instances of the first were certain towns and cities in classical Greece, the Roman Republic, a number of me-dieval Italian communes from about 1080 to 1300, and, provided one stretches the notion of popular government considerably, a few later republics that were, constitutionally speaking, less oligarchical than most, such as Geneva or perhaps Florence during some periods.

The second kind of regime first appeared, in incomplete form, in the United States, where many of its distinguishing features were already present early in the nineteenth century. However, most regimes of the second type have arisen in this century.

The two kinds of regime are substantially different both in ideals and in practices. If one were to read accounts of political ideals and neglect accounts of political practices, one might conclude that popular government on the small scale of the city-states came closer to realizing democratic potentialities than popular government on the large scale of the nation-state. However, historical accounts of actual practice, though lamentably incomplete (particularly for Greece), lend scant justification for idealizing actual political life in most city-states, including the ones mentioned above that were more democratized than most. The differences between the political institutions of the two kinds of popular regime are partly a function of the great difference in the scale of the city-state and the nation-state. Except for Rome, by modern standards the city-states were quite small both in population and territory. For example, of the fifteen leading city-states of Italy around 1300, when the influence of the *popolo* in the communes was at its zenith, the median population was around 38,000. New Zealand, one of the least populous democratic countries, has a hundred times more citizens than did fifth-century Athens or medieval Padua. In territory the difference in magnitude is even greater. The demos of the city-state was reduced still further by exclusion; for not only women were denied political rights, as later on they were in all countries until this century, but also a substantial part of the adult males. So the demos was always a minority of the adult population, and frequently a small minority at that. Consequently it is a mistake, though a common one, to regard the popular regimes of the city-states, including Athens, as examples of extensive popular participation in public affairs.

It is true that with the notable exception of Rome, after the republic extended beyond the city to the whole peninsula, the demos and the territory were generally small enough to allow the citizens to assemble as a body. Yet the conventional contrast between direct democracy in the city-state and representative democracy in the nation-state is also mistaken. To be sure, in Athens the assembly met often, and it may have exerted a good deal of influence on key decisions (though the slender evidence on that point could be read in different ways). But in the later city-states the popular assembly was much weaker (Hyde 1973, 54). As in modern countries, day-to-day government was in the hands of officials, who often made decisions of great consequence to the city. Here again Athens may have been exceptional in the extent to which citizens participated in political decisions, since many of its offices were filled by lot. In the medieval communes and later republics, however, officials were usually appointed or elected, and there was a marked tendency for officials to be chosen from the same leading families.

Despite the elected officials and councils, it is also true that neither in their ideas nor in their institutions did the city-states ever develop a legislature made up of representatives elected by the citizens. Without a system of representation, effective popular participation in large-scale government was impossible. Thus in the Roman Republic, participation was in practice limited to the tiny minority of citizens who could make their way to the capital city in order to attend the assemblies. Even if the idea of representation was not democratic in origin, it is no wonder that in the late eighteenth century, when advocates of popular government realized that representation might be joined with the democratic process to bring about democracy on the giant scale of an entire country, they saw this astounding new combination as among the greatest political inventions of all time.

It is true, finally, that the small scale of the city-state offered certain *possibilities* for political life that may be unattainable in the nation-state. Historians of political ideas like to contrast the naked pursuit of self and group interest in modern democratic countries with the ideal of an overarching common good that prevailed in ear-

9

lier political thought. The Italian civic humanists, for example, drew on Aristotle's theory of the *polis* to support their vision of the *vivere civile* as it could and should be (Pocock 1975, 74–75). Yet it is important not to confound these ideals with the actualities of political life in the city-states (Hale 1977, 43–75; Hyde 1973, 48–64; 104–123, 168–171; Martines 1979, 45–71, 148–161; Pullan 1972, 116–162). Their history is a tale of bitter conflicts and an almost total failure to develop effective institutions for settling political disputes by peaceful and constitutional means. Not only did they lack institutions for settling disputes between one city-state and another; they were not much better at settling internal conflicts, which erupted with great frequency along all the lines of cleavage so familiar today: family, kinship, neighborhood, occupation, class, religion. The outcome of political conflict was typically savage. Victors exiled or killed the losers, seized their property, and took vengeance on their kin. In this respect republics with popular governments were on the whole no better than the oligarchies and despotisms of their day.

As attempts were made during the last two centuries to extend democratic processes to the government of an entire country, it became evident that among a people unavoidably numerous and diverse, political conflict would be inescapable and might not be inherently undesirable. Because conflict was inevitable, it would express itself somehow. Is it not better to express it openly rather than stealthily? From assumptions like these it was a short step to the conclusion, which ran counter to the older republican tradition, that in a democratic country organized political parties and interest groups were necessary, normal, and desirable participants in political life.

Thus political institutions developed that, taken together, distinguish the political regimes of modern democratic countries from all other regimes, including those of the relatively democratized city-states. Seven institutions in particular, taken as a whole, define a type of regime that is historically unique:

1. Control over government decisions about policy is constitutionally vested in elected officials.

2. Elected officials are chosen in frequent and fairly conducted

elections in which coercion is comparatively uncommon.

3. Practically all adults have the right to vote in the election of officials.

4. Practically all adults have the right to run for elective offices in the government, though age limits may be higher for holding office than for the suffrage.

5. Citizens have a right to express themselves without the danger of severe punishment on political matters broadly defined, including criticism of officials, the government, the regime, the socioeconomic order, and the prevailing ideology.

6. Citizens have a right to seek out alternative sources of information. Moreover, alternative sources of information exist and are protected by law.

7. To achieve their various rights, including those listed above, citizens also have a right to form relatively independent associations or organizations, including independent political parties and interest groups.

Because these statements are meant to characterize actual and not merely nominal rights, institutions, and processes, they can also serve as criteria for distinguishing a special type of modern regime (Dahl 1971). Countries can be classified according to the extent to which their political institutions approximate these criteria. In ordinary usage, countries in which the political institutions most closely approximate these criteria are democratic. In order to emphasize the distinction between regimes like these and democracy in the ideal sense, they may also be called polyarchies. In this book I use several terms interchangeably: modern democratic systems, democratic regimes, democratic countries, large-scale democracy, polyarchy, and so on. None of these terms is meant to imply, of course, that these regimes are democratic in the ideal sense.

Like the regimes of the city-states, modern democratic regimes are far from satisfying the ideal democratic criteria. The gap between ideal and actual is partly the result of factors that are under human control and thus in principle could be remedied by human action. However, to apply democratic processes on a scale as large as a country also runs into certain inherent limits.

The Country as the Largest Feasible Democratic Unit

Two limits on democracy applied on a scale as large as a country are of special importance to the problem of democratic pluralism: the government of a country cannot be highly participatory, and the average citizen cannot have much influence over it.

Sometimes these limits are too casually brushed aside because democratic ideas came to the nation-state trailing clouds of glory from their infancy in the city-state. It is natural that the participatory ideal of the city-state, which its small size made theoretically possible even if the ideal was rarely if ever actualized, should cling to democracy in the nation-state. Yet in a country with a demos of only modest size, like Norway, and all the more in one as vast as the United States, the participatory ideal is impossible to attain, because the sheer numbers of persons impose requirements beyond the inexorable limits of a crucial resource which nature seems to have given us in fixed supply—time—and enormously increase all the other costs of communication and participation.

This is not to deny that levels of participation might be considerably higher than they are, nor that in many polyarchies, including the United States, existing patterns of participation tend to enhance the relative influence of the already advantaged strata. Yet even in optimal circumstances, in any system as large as a country the demos will be too large, with negligible exceptions, to permit the fulfillment of the participatory ideal.

Because of inherent limits on participation set by numbers, the average citizen in a nation-state (as Rousseau foresaw) cannot exercise as much influence on government as the average citizen of a much smaller unit might, at least in theory. Even though quantitative measures of influence are, as we shall see, more metaphor than metric, a one-millionth share in decision making, not to say a one-hundred-millionth share, cannot by any reasonable measure amount to much. Though voting is only one means by which a citizen may influence the government, it is the simplest and least costly in effort and individual resource; yet so slight is the effect of a single vote among a million or more others that in a large electorate it is questionable whether even the simple act of voting could be justified as a rational action by the individual voter. In any case, plainly in a large electorate a single voter can reasonably expect his vote to have only an infinitesimally small effect on the outcome. What is true of voting is a fortiori true of every other participatory action in which many citizens engage. To be sure, one person often exercises great influence not only because the number of people who participate in ways other than voting is small, but also because resources are unequally distributed and persons with superior resources employ them to enhance their influence. Inequalities in political resources could be reduced; at the theoretical limit they could be eliminated. But even perfect equality of influence could not overcome the limits of scale. In a large system, equality of influence would only mean that every citizen, not merely some citizens, would exercise an infinitesimally small amount of influence over the government.

For those who believe that the essential value of democracy is in the opportunities it offers individual citizens to participate in and exercise control over public life, the attempt to apply democratic processes on a scale as large as the nation-state is bound to produce a sorry substitute for the real thing. The high promise of democracy on the small scale of the city-state will remain forever unfulfilled in the nation-state and will remain so even if polyarchies become much more fully democratized than they are now.

Because of these (and no doubt other) inescapable shortcomings of large-scale democracy, it is frequently argued that democracy on a small scale should be strengthened. In appraising that argument, what are we to understand by the terms *small* and *large scale*? Limits on potentialities for participation and individual influence set in very swiftly as the number of citizens increases. A unit with a citizen body larger than a thousand, let us say, will drastically reduce opportunities for effective participation and individual influence. The precise number is arbitrary and the argument would not be affected if one were to raise the threshold to units with, say, ten thousand or even a hundred thousand citizens. The important point is that a reasonable upper limit on the meaning of the term *small-scale democracy* must refer to units very much smaller than any present country (except for a handful of microstates.) To anchor the notion more firmly, let me simply assume that by a small democracy we mean a unit with a population not more than a hundred thousand—a generous upper threshold that many advocates of small-scale democracy would consider ludicrously huge. To argue that small-scale democracy should be strengthened because there are inherent limits to democracy on a large scale may mean either of two things:

1. Democracy is desirable only on a small scale.
2. Within a system of large-scale democracy, smaller democratic units are also desirable.

Though advocates of small-scale democracy do not always distinguish these two positions, few people would accept the implications of the first. For the first argument implies either that political systems should not exist on a scale as large as a country or that although large political systems should exist, they should not be democratic. To defend the view that political systems should not exist on a large scale one would have to show how some of the most pressing problems of the modern world could be dealt with satisfactorily by small and totally independent systems—energy, pollution, social and economic disparities, defense, control of nuclear weapons, and so on. If large-scale political systems, such as countries, should exist to deal with problems like these, then to argue that they should not be democratized would require showing that undemocratic countries (a) would be better than relatively democratized countries, and (b) would permit small-scale democracies to exist.

Few advocates of small-scale democracy (I am one) would accept these implications. Certainly a good representative of that style of thought, the author of *Small Is Beautiful*, did not (Shumacher 1973, 228). I shall assume, therefore, that virtually all advocates of democracy today would agree with the second proposition. The argument then turns on the possibilities of strengthening smaller units or the democratic process in smaller units.

However, the reasons that justify the second proposition would also justify democracy on a scale larger than a single country. For just as units smaller than a country, though advantageous for some purposes, are too small to deal effectively with a number of crucial problems, so a single country has become too small a unit to secure economic well-being, security from nuclear war, and many other important goals. Consequently, it might be argued that transnational political systems should exist and that they should be democratized.

Of course, innumerable transnational organizations already exist, a few of which are by no means powerless: the European Community, NATO, COMECON, the U.N., not to mention the ubiquitous multinational corporations. However, none of these organizations is very democratic. Most are, at best, meritocracies exercising power delegated by policy-making institutions in member countries. Deficient as polyarchy may be in meeting the criteria for the democratic process, no international organization, at least none with any significant power to make decisions, remotely approaches polyarchy in meeting those criteria. In a sense so attenuated as to be virtually vacuous, the power of officials in the international organizations might be construed as having been "delegated" indirectly by the citizens of each country. But none of these organizations has a "people," a demos. Where, as in the European Community, there is a nascent demos, its representatives are weak. The European Community is the most likely collection of nations within which powerful transnational institutions will develop. Yet even there the development of federal institutions has been slow. It is difficult to foresee when, if ever, the Community may adopt a government nearly as democratic as the polyarchies now existing within the member countries. Even then, of course, the European Community would be far from all-inclusive; it would be no more than a supercountry, a federal Europe, with a population not much larger than that of the United States.

It seems, then, that today no unit smaller than a country can provide the conditions necessary for a good life, while no unit larger than a country is likely to be as democratically governed as a modern polyarchy. This is not to deny that units larger and smaller than a country are also required for a good life, nor that the extent of democracy attained in polyarchy is insufficient. It is only to say that a unit smaller than a country would be even less satisfactory in providing for a good life, while a unit larger than a country would be even less satisfactory as a democratic system. Consequently, my treatment of the problem of democratic pluralism will apply primarily to countries rather than the smaller units within countries, or to microstates, or to larger transnational organizations.

Political Autonomy and Control

The plausibility of the proposition that relatively autonomous organizations exist in all democratic countries depends on two different kinds of judgments, one primarily semantic, the other primarily empirical. Distinguishing the two kinds of judgments will help us to avoid the trap of making that proposition either logically true or false by definition, or empirically true or false in a trivial way. I want now to explore a way of thinking about the meaning of political autonomy (independence) that will help us to avoid these errors.

As a first cut, let me propose that to be autonomous in a political sense is to be not under the control of another. Political autonomy is the complement of control: Beta's decision to act in some way—call it action x—is politically autonomous in relation to another actor Alpha, to the extent that Alpha does not control Beta's doing x. Since political autonomy in this sense can also be called independence, I shall use these two terms interchangeably.

By control I mean a relation among actors such that the preferences, desires, or intentions of one or more actors bring about conforming actions, or predispositions to act, of one or more other actors. Control is thus a causal relationship: the actions of one actor are interpreted as having been brought about, or caused by, the preferences of other actors. For example, Alpha's desires cause Beta to do x, or intend to do x, or acquire a predisposition for doing x.

Neighboring Concepts

Since attempts to clarify the meaning of terms like *power, influence*, and *control* have produced an overabundance of names and definitions, let me draw some boundaries around the meaning of control that distinguish it from certain other neighboring concepts.

To begin with, control is not equivalent to benefits. The distinction needs to be emphasized, since some writers propose to identify power with benefits: if Alpha derives benefits from Beta's actions, then Alpha must have power over Beta. It is sometimes unclear whether benefits are meant to be identical with power or whether instead benefits are simply meant to be a surrogate for power, an operational indicator employed on the assumption that power and benefits are always strictly correlated. In either case, to stipulate that power and benefits are equivalent can prove seriously misleading: American wheat farmers can benefit from a decision of the Soviet leaders to buy American grain, but they can hardly be said to control the Soviet leaders in their decision to buy American grain. Convenient as it may be to measure power by benefits, to do so would settle a difficult empirical question by a simple definitional fiat. The question is—and would remain—how power and control are related to benefits like income, wealth, and social status.

Control is also both more inclusive and less inclusive than certain other concepts. Thus control need not be intentional; it may also be unintentional. Although Beta's action x must be brought about by Alpha's preferences, desire, or intentions, Alpha need not specifically desire or *intend* that Beta do x. What is crucial is that Alpha wants x to occur (or wants the results of x), and that, as a result, Beta does x. Alpha need not even know that Beta exists. When managers of firms try to satisfy consumer preferences in a competitive market, consumers control some of the firms' actions without necessarily intending to do so. A representative who assiduously studies public opinion in his constituency and attempts to follow majority views in voting on legislation is to this extent controlled by his constituents, even though they may have no particular intention that he vote one way or another on particular bills.

At the same time, however, control is narrower than influence, at least in the broad meaning of influence. If Alpha controls Beta with respect to x, it is necessarily true that Alpha influences Beta with respect to x. But Alpha may influence Beta's doing x and not control Beta. Influence thus includes a broader area of causation than control. For control is limited to relations in which Beta's actions or predispositions are in conformity with Alpha's preferences, desires, or intentions. Control therefore excludes "negative" influence, as when Beta adopts the principle "If Alpha's for it, I'm against it." Control is also meant to exclude Alpha's influence on Beta if Beta's actions cannot reasonably be said to be caused by Alpha's preferences, desires, or intentions. Thus if workers at General Electric seek unemployment benefits—because G.E. has laid them off; because sales of transistor radios are down; because imports from Taiwan, Hong Kong, and South Korea are cheaper; because workers in those places work harder at lower wages—it is perfectly appropriate to say that the actions of G.E. workers are influenced by the actions of workers (and employers, of course) in Taiwan, Hong Kong, and South Korea, but we could not say that in seeking unemployment benefits G.E. workers are *controlled* by workers in Taiwan and elsewhere. For it is unreasonable to attribute to workers in Taiwan or elsewhere the desire or intention that G.E. workers seek unemployment benefits or even that they be laid off from their jobs.

What about the influence of social structures—constitutions, economic orders, educational arrangements, status systems, penal systems, and so on? To ignore their impact would be to omit influences of extraordinary importance, since much of what people do is influenced by the restraints and opportunities provided by social structures. But are we to attribute preferences, desires, or intentions to social structures and if not, how are we to describe their influence? Consider two possibilities:

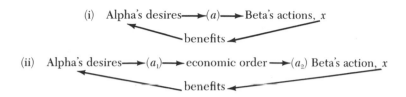

(i) Alpha's desires——▶(a)——▶Beta's actions, x
◀————benefits◀————

(ii) Alpha's desires——▶(a₁)——▶economic order——▶(a₂) Beta's action, x
◀————benefits◀————

In both instances, Beta's actions benefit Alpha. The first is by defini-tion a case of Alpha controlling Beta. How shall we describe the sec-ond? It seems reasonable enough to describe (a_1) as an instance of Alpha exercising control over the economic structure: we simply treat the structure as in some sense an actor. But to attribute prefer-ences, desires, or intentions to an economic structure is an exces-sive reification. Strictly speaking, then, (a_2) is not an instance of control. Yet it is obviously a close neighbor and a mighty potent neighbor at that. I propose to call (a_2) an example of *social regula-tion*. Thus in describing (ii) I shall say that Beta's action is *regulated* by the economic order, which is *controlled* by Alpha, who *benefits* from Beta's action. The economic order, then, might be called a regulative structure. The terms help to distinguish phenomena that are sometimes lumped together.

By bringing social regulation and regulative structures into the picture, however, we create a paradox about autonomy. Since politi-cal autonomy has been defined as the complement of control, not regulation, by definition Beta's action in (ii) is independent of social structure. Clearly this is an abuse of language and common sense. Consequently, I propose to call the complement of social regulation *social* autonomy (or *social* independence).

It is a tantalizing question whether between them control and social regulation exhaust the space available for human autonomy. I think not; there may yet be room for "personal," "moral," or "psy-chological" autonomy. But if so, that space must be vastly shrunken. However, these notions of autonomy are beyond my purview here. Perhaps it is sufficient to suggest that political autonomy in my sense appears roughly equivalent to Sir Isaiah Berlin's concept of negative liberty, and control to his positive liberty. Unlike Berlin, however, I would be inclined to say that in order to be free one must be able to exercise both autonomy and control; yet in order for everyone to be maximally free, no person's political autonomy or control can be unlimited. Is this perhaps only another way of stating the problem of democratic pluralism? I must admit also that if autonomy hinges on control and control is a form of causation, then we march more and more deeply into the realm of the problematical. As everyone knows, the idea of causation is jam-packed with difficulties, which are compounded when causal explanation extends to human actions. Nonetheless, causal thinking enables us not only to orient ourselves toward the world but also to act in and upon the world, to seize hold of certain levers in order to achieve our purposes. By understanding causes sometimes we can bring about effects. Even though freedom and causality are irreducible antinomies, I do not see how we could act freely without understanding causes.

Dimensions of Political Autonomy

Like control, political autonomy or independence begins to take on meaning as it is described in context. It is not very helpful to treat political autonomy as if it were a universal or fixed property of human beings, or even of all the members of a particular society, country, organization, or other aggregate. Like control, autonomy always implies a relation between specific actors, whether individual persons or aggregates of persons. In the simplest possible relation, autonomy like control is a dyadic relation: Beta is autonomous in relation to Alpha. As with causation generally, however, control and autonomy need not be and frequently are not dyadic. Beta's action may be controlled by many actors and not just Alpha; Alpha may control not only Beta but many others, and so on, to an indefinite degree of complexity. Furthermore, though it is helpful to think of the actors as individual persons, actors may be aggregates. Beta may be a class of slaves, Alpha a class of slave owners.

Ordinarily, to identify the actors involved in a relation of control or autonomy is not enough. If we are told that Alpha controls

Beta we will want to ask, With respect to what, exactly? So with autonomy: It is usually not of much interest to know that Beta is independent of Alpha in some way. If it is a matter of Beta's independence in the way he combs his hair, we may not much care. Just as Alpha controls Beta with respect to some particular category of actions, so too with the mirror image of influence, autonomy: in relation to Alpha, Beta is autonomous with respect to some category of actions. Beta's action x can be anything humanly possible, individual or collective: wearing the latest fashions, concealing or speaking one's thoughts about the boss, voting, going on strike, supporting a revolution, paring one's fingernails frequently. Just as we might define the *range* of Alpha's influence over Beta as all the categories of Beta's actions influenced by Alpha, so the *range* of Beta's autonomy in relation to Alpha consists of all the categories of actions not influenced by Alpha. It follows, of course, that Beta may be independent of Alpha with respect to some particular category of action, y, but not with respect to another category of action, x. And with respect to y, Beta may be independent of Alpha, but under the control of Gamma.

A problem remains. How are we to describe the magnitude of Alpha's control over Beta and others, and thus the autonomy of Beta and others in relation to Alpha? Crudely, is Alpha's autonomy large or trivially small? Alas, satisfactory measures for describing amounts of influence, control, power, and so on are much more elusive than quantitative measures for describing wealth and income. For all their shortcomings, acceptable measures do exist for describing wealth and income; and because for many purposes we can describe Alpha's income and wealth by numerical quantities, we can also describe meaningfully how income and wealth are distributed among a set of actors, say the inhabitants of the United States. By contrast, no acceptable way of describing magnitudes of influence, control, or power exists, even though a number of theoretical measures, some of great elegance, have been proposed.

In discussing the distribution of power, influence, or control, then, quantitative terms tend to become metaphors rather than measures. Nonetheless, I believe that it helps one to perceive and to describe social relations more accurately if we think about "amounts" of influence and autonomy *as if* they could vary—like income and wealth—over an indefinitely large range of values.

Because everyday language indicates that many of us do think this way some of the time, to recommend the use of quantitative metaphors in describing control and autonomy may strike some readers as too obvious to need saying. The fact is, however, that not everyone does think about the matter in this way. Some writers have conceived of power—and by implication what I mean by autonomy and control—as if it could be described by only two quantities: all or none. Although this is far from the prevailing view, it offers such a strong contrast to the interpretation suggested here that to consider it briefly may be illuminating.

Power as Domination
Instead of conceiving of control varying over an indefinite range of magnitudes, in one alternative view power is either present or absent; if present it is total. In this sense, the amount of power any actor can exercise is all or nothing, 100 percent or zero. This solution was advanced by Ralf Dahrendorf in *Class and Class Conflict in Industrial Society* (1959). Although Dahrendorf managed to arrive essentially at a pluralist interpretation of postcapitalist society, his point of departure made the voyage unusually difficult. Later, Isaac Balbus (1971) adapted Dahrendorf's concept in the course of a critique of pluralism from a Marxist perspective.

Although Dahrendorf and Balbus do not deal with autonomy, the implications of their analysis for autonomy (in the sense used here) are quite clear: if, like power, control is all or nothing, then political autonomy must also be all or nothing. If Alpha exercises any control over Beta, then Beta can have no autonomy at all. Though their framework does not provide for distinctions as to category and range, one might interpret them less broadly as intending to say that if Alpha exercises any control over Beta with respect to x, then Beta has no autonomy in relation to Alpha with respect to x.

The principal objections to their postulate are three: First, as a theoretical assumption the postulate is highly arbitrary. If we had at hand a widely applicable means of measuring power, it is hard to imagine that anyone would settle for anything so arbitrary as the theoretical assumption that power allows only two possibilities. Second, such a formulation loses most of its meaning unless the terms *domination* and *subjection*, which carry extremely harsh overtones, are carefully defined. Yet neither writer gave the words concrete meaning. (I do so in the next chapter.) Finally, to interpret control, power, or authority as consisting *only* of domination and subjection hinders rather than facilitates one's understanding of the world and its possibilities. In this view, the world offers us only three possibilities for social existence: dominate, be dominated, or withdraw into total isolation. Since the last is hardly possible and surely undesirable, the options are reduced to domination and subjection. All cooperation, all reciprocity, all mutual control, is nothing more than the predator and its quarry. By definition we are forever denied the very possibility of mutual controls, which appear to offer the main hope for humane systems of authority. Neither Dahrendorf, a democratic pluralist, nor Balbus, a Marxist, could have intended us to accept such a bleak and pessimistic view of human possibilities.

Sources of Conflicting Judgments
It is one thing to think about autonomy and control as varying in magnitude like income and wealth over an indefinitely large range of values, but it is quite another to describe concrete control relations. Descriptions may, and do, conflict, not only because of differences in empirical observations and inferences but also because of difficulties in the concept of control itself (and presumably also in all related concepts such as power, influence, and so on).

First, observers may disagree in describing the magnitude of Alpha's control over Beta specifically *with respect to* x. How great is the control of major oil companies over congressional energy legislation? Not only would an answer require one to appraise a vast body of complex information (some not readily available, if at all), but in the absence of an acceptable measure of magnitudes, different observers are likely to reach different qualitative judgments. Second, observers may disagree in judging the relative weight to be given one kind of action as compared with another. If Alpha controls Beta with respect to x and Gamma with respect to y, is x as important as y? More? Less? When different actors and different sets of actions are involved, judgments become even more controversial. Third, observers may disagree about where to locate the appropriate boundaries of a description. The autonomy we attribute to Beta in doing y might diminish if we were to take more actors into account. If we cast our net widely enough to include all the actors who have influenced Beta, perhaps Beta's independence would vanish entirely. Indeed, to one who believes that all human actions are fully determined, Beta's political autonomy is an illusion; every description of Beta as acting independently is simply an error resulting from faulty language, methodology, or information. Even if we chose not to destroy political autonomy simply by adopting the postulate of determinism, a description of Beta's political autonomy may change drastically depending on the set of actors included among the causes of Beta's actions.

Imagine an extremely simple system involving only three actors, Alpha, Beta, and Gamma, whose relations—quite unrealistically—all run one way. In increasing order of their "directness," five direct causes are Beta's life experiences, his character or personality, his "consciousness," the agenda of choices he perceives in a particular situation, and his preferences among the choices on his agenda. In addition to these characteristics of Beta are the influences of the other actors in Beta's social space, who are influenced in turn by their own life experiences, and so on. Somewhat more remote in time are the recent collective experiences of the aggregates of which Beta is a part, like the residual effects of the Vietnam War on Americans; widely prevailing civic orientations that condition Beta's perceptions, such as racial attitudes or prevailing beliefs about capitalism, socialism, and democracy; and key social structures, like the constitutional system of the government of the state, the hierarchic government of firms, the market, and so on. Obviously each of these very general categories is also a result of other causes still more remote in time: earlier historical experiences, like the American Civil War, the Constitutional Convention, the American Revolution, the Colonial period, and so on; earlier prevailing civic orientations, such as the Protestant ethic, or the passion for equality that Tocqueville described; and earlier structures, such as slavery, widespread ownership of farms, and so on.

Thus the boundaries around an account of why Beta does x are not rigidly fixed by some palpable phenomenon revealed by our senses, like a chain-wire fence around a factory. Instead the boundaries are creations of the human mind—more like the boundaries the ancients drew around the constellations they saw in the heavens on clear nights. Where one decides to draw boundaries around a causal system that is intended to explain human actions seems to depend in a significant way on many factors, including one's curiosities, purposes, and prior judgments as to the usefulness of a particular bit of additional knowledge. In order to answer the persistent Why? one may be challenged to move from one region of explanation to another. Where one stops in the search for conclusive answers will depend on contestable judgments as to what one thinks it is crucial to explain, and how far outward in time and social space one wants to explore in search of a satisfactory account. To be sure, one may finally arrive at a boundary where the causal system is closed, in the sense that no further factors need to be taken into account in order wholly to explain the outcome. But when significant human actions are to be accounted for, complete closure is sure to require a vast system.

These difficulties could result in conflicting descriptions of activities. As descriptions move toward more remote causes, they are increasingly difficult to confirm or falsify and more and more dependent on one's interpretative assumptions, including a priori judgments as to the validity of the theory in which the explanation itself is grounded. Thus theory runs the risk of self-confirmation.

It is because of these and other sources of conflicting and not easily resolvable judgments that the proposition this chapter began with probably cannot be conclusively demonstrated as true or false. And that is why I offer it as an assumption. Whether one accepts or rejects the premise that independent organizations exist in all democratic countries will probably depend less on any account I might set forth, even if this book were entirely given over to such an effort, than to one's prior judgment. What I have tried to do in this section is to clarify the meaning of the premise, as well as other statements about autonomy and control elsewhere in this book, and to insure that I have not made the premise true or false largely by definition.

Yet if I have now escaped the trap of definitional triviality, the possibility remains that the premise is empirically true or false in a trivial way. Consider: If a system can be described as pluralist whenever any organization possesses some political autonomy, then are not all political systems pluralist, even totalitarian regimes? The totalitarian model is after all an abstraction; in practice, probably no regime has ever deprived all organizations of all their independence on all matters. Conversely, if in order to qualify as pluralist all the important organizations in a system must be fully independent of all controls, then no regime could ever be described as pluralist. (Indeed, one would not even want to call a collection of fully independent organizations a *system.*)

I propose therefore to define *relative autonomy* as follows: An organization is relatively autonomous if it undertakes actions that (a) are considered harmful by another organization and that (b) no other organization, including the government of the state, can prevent, or could prevent except by incurring costs so high as to exceed the gains to the actor from doing so. Judgments about harm, costs, and gains are not entirely objective or fixed. However, let me describe some organizations that are, I believe, relatively autonomous in all democratic countries.

Organizations

The word *organization* is perhaps a trifle too hard-edged. Rousseau, who was deeply worried about the presence of independent organizations within the state, called them *partial* or *particular societies*. Tocqueville called them *associations*, and praised them (though not without qualification) as necessary to a people who wished to enjoy not only democracy and equality but also liberty and civilization. The word *groups* will often serve, and in some contexts it is helpful to use a term of recent vintage and refer to them as *subsystems*.

Of organizations, partial societies, associations, groups, and subsystems there is no end, and in various times and places diverse associations have claimed a measure of independence from the state and other associations. Probably the most ancient to claim rightful standing as a partly autonomous association consists of a group of people who are closely affiliated by virtue of their kinship bonds, such as the family. Although extreme authoritarians have sometimes seen the family as the penultimate link in a hierarchical chain extending unbroken from ruler to subject, more commonly the inner life of the family has been thought to require some freedom from state control. Familial bonds are exceptionally tough, and even in the most despotic regimes intimate kinship groups seem to have retained some autonomy.

Some of the family's area of independence from the state has generally been taken over by religious organizations, which in turn have usually insisted on their own sphere of autonomy within the state, even when church and state are allies. Educational, scientific, and cultural associations, and in Europe since the middle ages universities, have frequently managed to gain some independence from the state.

Associations like these, based on kinship, religion, and cultural life, are, however, less central to the problem of autonomy and control in modern democratic orders than certain other kinds of organizations that I am going to lump into three untidy heaps, on which I want to stick the labels governmental, political, and economic. As to the first, whatever constitutional theory may prescribe, in every democratic country the major institutions of government—the chief executive, the bureaucracies, the parliament, the judiciary— are in important respects independent of one another. Although the legislature and the chief executive are probably more independent of one another in countries where the doctrine of separation of powers is explicitly enshrined in constitutional theory and practice (like the United States), some independence exists among the major institutions of the national government in all democratic countries today. In addition, in every democratic country local governments enjoy some degree of independence. While the autonomy of states, provinces, regions, or cantons is no doubt greater in countries with federal constitutions, in all democratic countries local governments are in practice, if not in constitutional theory, more than merely bureaucratic arms of the national government.

Interacting in complex ways with governmental organizations are a great variety of political associations, particularly political parties and interest groups. Viewed from a historical or comparative perspective, the claim that the political order ought to permit independent political parties and interest groups to exist has been much more often denied than granted. But the extent of independence permitted to parties and interest groups is a characteristic of modern democratic regimes that distinguishes them not only from authoritarian regimes but from republics of earlier times like Venice. What for centuries was held to be the lethal poison of republics, the spirit of faction, is in modern democracies institutionalized in parties and interest groups.

Economic organizations, mainly business firms and trade unions, are also deeply implicated in the problem of autonomy and control. Their autonomy is at once a fact, a value, and a source of harm. In all democratic countries, business firms make important decisions that are not fully controlled by government officials; even state-owned firms usually enjoy a significant measure of autonomy in relation to parliament, cabinet, and central bureaucracies. Probably no one would deny that their actions are sometimes harmful.

Consequently, their autonomy has met steady opposition. Although socialists and other critics of business have often contended that their harm could be minimized by greater state control, in recent years more and more advocates of democratic socialism have concluded that centralized state socialism is likely to be not only inefficient but also inhumane and undemocratic as well. Consequently, many socialists now advocate some system of decentralized socialism with socially owned but relatively autonomous enterprises. I want therefore to suggest, in passing, a point I shall explain in more detail later on: a decentralized socialist order would have its own problems with autonomy and control.

Independent trade unions that exercise the right to strike exist in all democratic countries. Indeed, it has been argued that collective bargaining backed up by the right to strike is essential to a democratic order. However that may be, the right to strike is protected in all democratic countries. In exercising the right to strike, trade unions are relatively autonomous in relation both to employers and to the government itself. Though employers usually foresee serious harm from strikes, they are unable to prevent their organized workers from striking. Even governments frequently find themselves without sufficient power to prevent unions from engaging in strikes and negotiating contracts contrary to government policy—sometimes even contrary to law.

Conclusion and Premise

Of the more than one hundred and fifty countries in the world today, the institutions of polyarchy exist in about thirty. In these countries, some important governmental, political, and economic organizations are relatively autonomous in relation to one another. In this sense, then, all democratic countries are also pluralist.

To avoid misunderstanding, let me point out that not all pluralist systems are democratic: relatively autonomous organizations also exist under some nondemocratic regimes. Nor are all democratic systems necessarily pluralist: democracy might conceivably exist on a very small scale without relatively autonomous subsystems, as Rousseau seems to have hoped. However, all large-scale democratic systems, all democratic countries, all polyarchies, are organizationally pluralist in the meaning of the terms I have tried to clarify in this chapter.

If all democratic countries are organizationally pluralist, then the problem of democratic pluralism exists in all democratic countries: it is a universal problem in modern democracy. I now want to describe the problem itself in more detail.

3

The Problem of Pluralist Democracy

To hold that a plurality of important and relatively autonomous organizations exists in democratic countries does not imply that their existence creates a serious problem. If the consequences of organizational pluralism were entirely advantageous, there would be no problem; if, though disadvantages existed, they were minuscule in comparison with the advantages, the problem would not be serious; while if independent organizations could easily be eliminated without doing much harm, the problem could easily be solved. The problem of democratic pluralism is serious, however, precisely because independent organizations are highly desirable and at the same time their independence allows them to do harm.

Why Independent Organizations Are Desirable

Writers like Durkheim and the early legal pluralists stressed that associations are essential to basic human needs for sociability, intimacy, affection, friendship, love, trust, and faith; for individual growth, personal integrity, and socialization into community norms; for the preservation and transmission of culture; for the human qualities of human beings. Tocqueville and others have argued that associations are also essential to freedom.

These are, I believe, valid arguments. More germane to the problem of democratic pluralism are two other reasons why relatively independent organizations are desirable.

For Mutual Control

In large political systems independent organizations help to prevent domination and to create mutual control. The main alternative to mutual control in the government of the state is hierarchy. To govern a system as large as a country exclusively by hierarchy is to invite domination by those who control the government of the state. Independent organizations help to curb hierarchy and domination.

Obvious as this conclusion may appear, it stands in fundamental contradiction to the views of social theorists who contend that domination is inevitable. Two bodies of thought portraying domination as inherent in all political systems—up to the present, at least—have been particularly influential. In standard Marxism, a bourgeois society is necessarily dominated by a minority consisting of an exploitative capitalist class. However, in this view domination is not inherent in social existence but is destined to be superseded by freedom and mutuality when capitalism is replaced by socialism. The theories of elite rule developed by Pareto, Mosca, and Michels are far more pessimistic. In their view, domination by a minority—whether a class, an elite, or a social stratum—is inherent in large-scale society. Thus, this trio of elite theorists transformed Marx's profound optimism into an equally profound pessimism.

Whether we choose to accept the view that domination is inherent in social existence, or would vanish under socialism, obviously depends in part on what we understand the term to mean. In the last chapter, I offered reasons for rejecting one version of domination that depended for its validity more on definition than on observation and analysis. Yet, it would be possible to commit the opposite error of ruling out domination by definition. A tendency toward dominance has been so widely described by social theorists, however, that we cannot dismiss it as groundless or without meaning. Suppose therefore that we try to capture the meaning of this slippery term by adopting something like this: Alpha dominates Beta if Alpha's control (a) is strictly unilateral, (b) persists over a relatively long period of time, (c) extends over a range of actions of great importance to Beta, and (d) compels Beta to act in ways that on balance are costly to her. Now, imagine a system in which rulers dominate their subjects on conditions of work, let us say, or political and religious beliefs and practices, or access to the means of production, or laws defining crime and punishment, or the conditions of access to an education, or all of these things and more. The question arises: Could subjects possibly transform such a system of domination into a system of mutual (though not necessarily equal, fair, or democratic) controls with respect to important matters like these?

Views of domination like those found in standard Marxism and Italian elite theory are surely correct in emphasizing the strength and universality of tendencies toward domination. Where these views go wrong is in underestimating the strength of tendencies toward political autonomy and mutual control. Throughout history, relatively autonomous organizations have developed around certain universal human situations that generate common experiences, identifications, and values: we and they, insider and outsider, friend and enemy, sacred and profane, true believer and infidel, civilized man and barbarian. Kinship, language, birthplace, residence, religion, occupation, everywhere stimulate a thrust toward organization and independence. Alongside Michels's famous iron law of oligarchy—"Who says organization says oligarchy"—stands another: Every organization develops an impulse toward its own independence. The two universal tendencies are alloyed; and in the alloy, the law of oligarchy bends more easily than iron.

Less metaphorically, subjects can sometimes gain a degree of independence from their rulers on matters of importance to themselves if they can make the costs of domination so high that domination no longer looks worthwhile to the rulers. Resources are not infinite after all, and exercising control nearly always requires an outlay of resources. Domination, it is fair to say, always does. Thus, control is almost always to some extent costly to the ruler; and domination is sure to be—though it may be cheap, it does not come free. Rulers therefore have to decide when and whether the game of domination is worth the candle. Sometimes it is not.

In describing how this might come about, it is useful to imagine that the ruler is at least moderately rational. A ruler whose actions were directed only to maximizing his own goals and were rationally calculated would not commit his resources beyond the point at which the value of the benefits he expected to gain were exceeded by the costs. The value of control might be defined as the excess of expected benefits over expected costs. If the costs of control exceed the benefits, then effective control in that range or domain has no value to the ruler. Confronted by the prospect that the costs of control were going to exceed the benefits, even rulers with great but finite resources would rationally forego the full attainment of their goals in order to exercise control within the limits of their resources. Rational rulers would allocate their finite resources among goals so as to maximize the net benefits (as evaluated from the perspective of their goals). Wherever the costs of control exceeded the benefits, it would be rational for these rulers to reduce costs by leaving some actions beyond their control, leaving some matters outside their control, or accepting a higher level of unreliability and unpredictability in their control. For the subjects, of course, the trick is to raise the costs of domination and thus reduce its value to the rulers.

Fine in theory, one might object, but what about the poor devil whose neck is squarely under the ruler's heel? To contend that subjects can always escape domination would be witless. Nonetheless, a variety of factors do, at times, enable subjects to raise the costs of domination. To begin with, it is virtually impossible for a single actor or a unified team to acquire a complete monopoly over all resources. Consequently, subjects nearly always have access to *some* resources, however pitiful they may be. Moreover, subjects can sometimes cooperate, combine their resources, and thus increase the costs of control. In addition, rulers are rarely a solidary group. Although each member of a dominant elite may have an interest in maintaining the elite's domination over the rest of the society, and so too an interest in walling off internal disputes from outsiders, security around the wall is not always perfectly tight and traffic through it may be mutually profitable. If some outsiders have resources that might be thrown into the struggle, their help could be crucial to the victory of a faction within the walls.

For reasons like these, subjects can sometimes push the costs of control over certain matters to a point where rulers no longer find it worthwhile to try to dominate their subjects on these particular questions. Subjects thus acquire a degree of political autonomy. The change toward religious toleration in Europe after the bloody and destructive religious conflicts of the sixteenth and seventeenth centuries reflected an appreciation by monarchs that the gains from enforced religious conformity were very much smaller than had been supposed, the costs were very much greater, and on balance, the costs greatly exceeded the gains. In the sixteenth and seventeenth centuries, neither emperor nor pope succeeded in dominating all the city states of northern Italy. In their desire for independence, the city-states made outside domination too costly, despite the superior resources—in gross—of the two main contenders. In Britain, Sweden, Norway, and the Netherlands, parliaments gained independence from domination by centralized monarchies. In the eighteenth century, the growing acceptance of organized political oppositions in Britain reflected a fundamentally changed perspective in which—as with religion earlier—the costs expected from tolerating political opponents declined while the costs expected from repression increased. In the nineteenth and early twentieth centuries, workers combined their meager resources in trade unions and successfully overthrew the unilateral domination of employers over wages, hours, and working conditions.

One could endlessly multiply historical examples showing how members of a weaker group have combined their resources, raised the costs of control, overcome domination on certain matters important to them, and acquired some measure of political autonomy. Often what results is a system of mutual controls. Thus, after parliament gained independence from the monarch, for a long time neither could dominate the other; each partly controlled the other in important ways. Later, mutual controls developed between cabinet and parliament; later still, between parliament and electorate. And even later, the rise of independent trade unions helped to bring about mutual controls between unions and employers.

Thus domination can be transformed into a system of mutual controls. Lest one exaggerate the possibility, however, let me sound several cautionary notes. While domination is not inherent in social existence, subjects cannot always bring domination to an end: ask prisoners in concentration camps whether they can overthrow their jailers. Moreover, while Michels exaggerated the strength of the iron law, the tendency toward oligarchy is always there. An organization that successfully prevents domination by outsiders may provide the means, as Michels rightly saw, by which its own leaders now dominate its members. Nor is mutual control equivalent to equitable control, much less to equal or democratic control. To say, then, that independent organizations help to prevent domination and bring about mutual control is not to say that they guarantee justice, equality, or democracy. A political system can be pluralist and yet lack democratic institutions. Nondemocratic systems can contain important organizations that are relatively autonomous vis-à-vis the government of the state; some authoritarian countries do.

For Democracy on a Large Scale

Yet, while relatively autonomous organizations are not sufficient for democracy per se, they are a necessary element in a large-scale democracy, both as a prerequisite for its operation and as an inevitable consequence of its institutions.

The rights required for democracy on a large scale make relatively autonomous organizations simultaneously possible and necessary. For example, elections cannot be contested in a large system without organizations. To forbid political parties would make it impossible for citizens to coordinate their efforts in order to nominate and elect their preferred candidates and thus would violate the criteria of voting equality and effective participation. To forbid all political parties save one would be to grant exceptional opportunities to the members of the one party in comparison with other citizens.

To prohibit citizens from organizing freely in order to make their views known to legislators and to other citizens would violate the criteria of effective participation and enlightened understanding, and it would mock the idea of final control over the agenda by the citizen body. Thus the introduction of democratic processes into the government of a country and the enforcement of the rights required if democratic procedures are to be effectively protected make it both possible and advantageous for various groups to form autonomous organizations. Because organizations are possible and advantageous, they are also inevitable.

From the perspective of the previous section, the institutions of polyarchy make organizations possible in a democratic country, because they impose very high costs on efforts to destroy the relative autonomy of organizations that are formed to contest the government's conduct. Where the institutions have gained widespread support, as they generally have in countries with long-established systems of polyarchy, the costs of suppression far outstrip the likely gains even for the most influential actors with the greatest access to political resources, that is, the political elites. If the institutions of polyarchy in a country make it possible for groups to form autonomous organizations, they also make it advantageous to do so—not least for the political elites themselves. In particular, as elites discovered comparatively early in the development of polyarchal institutions, in order to exert maximum influence on the conduct, policies, personnel, and structure of government by competing for office in elections or by affecting the chances that a legislator (or a popularly elected executive) will be reelected, it is highly advantageous to organize political parties and pressure groups. Once parties and pressure groups exist, no elite groups can suppress them without destroying the institutions that distinguish polyarchy from more authoritarian regimes. Indeed, one of the first acts of a new authoritarian regime is generally to suppress all opposition parties; one of the first acts of a regime formed to institute democracy is to allow parties to exist.

Nor is autonomy limited only to organizations that, like parties, are explicitly political. Democratic countries are distinguished by a general freedom to form and join organizations—religious, cultural, intellectual, labor, agricultural, commercial, professional. Only the slightest diversity is needed to make it seem advantageous to some persons to cooperate in subsystems that are independent in some respects from the government of the state and from other organizations. The social thrust toward organization intensifies as consciousness grows of the advantages to be gained from cooperation and from pooling resources. In modern countries, there is a highly developed sense of the advantages of organization; this sense is, in fact, one characteristic of what we mean by modernity. In any modern country, then, organizations are bound to proliferate unless they are stamped out by coercion. To suppress the astonishing number and variety of autonomous organizations that spring to life in a modern country, then, organizations are bound to proliferate unless they are stamped out by coercion. To suppress the astonishing number trol at the center. Because it is in democratic countries that the existence of independent organizations is most fully protected by the institutions of the regime, it is in democratic countries that they flourish.

Are statements like these more than mere conjectures? Let me suggest a two-stage test: first a mental experiment, then some specific experience. For our mental experiment, let us imagine a country with remarkable diversity among its people on a very considerable number of characteristics: language, religion, ideology, region, ethnic group, national identification, race . . . Suppose, however, that these differences did not manifest themselves in political conflict. To prevent these cleavages in political life requires a regime, we shall suppose, in which a small set of unified rulers can mobilize an overwhelming preponderance of political resources for their own use and for maintaining a severely hierarchical bureaucracy, and can deny to everyone else practically all access to political resources. Given a highly authoritarian regime of this kind, little or no overt conflict appears, and the latent pattern of conflict remains unmanifest in political life.

Let us now imagine that the barriers to oppositions are gradually reduced. Is it not reasonable to expect that as the barriers go down, relatively autonomous organizations will spring up, and that some of these organizations will seek to advance the claims of the hitherto politically latent groups and subcultures? Would we not expect that, up to some point, the more the barriers to organization and participation are reduced, the greater will be the proliferation of relatively autonomous organizations, and that, in time, patterns of considerable durability will emerge?

Fortunately, historical experience provides us with events that are as close to an actual testing of our mental experiment as we are ever likely to have in political life. For something very much like this occurred in Italy, Austria, Germany, and Japan after the displacement of authoritarian regimes in those countries as a result of military action in World War II. Or to take another example, de-Stalinization in Yugoslavia after 1950 led to a great multiplicity of interest groups, even though the end-point fell short of polyarchy. In Czechoslovakia during the famous Prague Spring of 1968, a rich organizational life sprang abruptly into existence. More recently, democratization and liberalization of authoritarian regimes in Portugal and Spain have had the same consequences.

Like a film running backward, the process has also occurred when some group has established hegemonic control over the government, destroyed all autonomous organizations, prevented the manifestation of public conflict, and built a hierarchical structure of order over the remains of the silenced opposition. So it was in Chile after the destruction of polyarchy by the military. Indeed, so it had been earlier in Italy, Germany, Austria, and Japan; and so, too, it came about in Czechoslovakia when the Prague Spring was brought to an end by the Soviet military invasion.

In the same country, in a period of time too short for significant changes to occur in the latent pattern of social cleavages, changes in regime have resulted in enormous changes in the amount of organizational pluralism. Consequently, it is scarcely open to reasonable doubt that organizational pluralism is a concomitant, both as cause and effect, of the liberalization and democratization of hegemonic regimes.

Defects in Pluralist Democracy

Desirable as independent organizations are for these reasons, they also appear to be implicated in four problems of democratic pluralism: they may help to stabilize injustices, deform civic consciousness, distort the public agenda, and alienate final control over the agenda.

Stabilizing Political Inequalities

Even when the institutional guarantees of polyarchy exist and the political system of a country is democratic to this extent, organizational pluralism is perfectly consistent with extensive inequalities.* Moreover, the influence and power of organizations does more than simply register existing inequalities in other resources. Organization is itself a resource. It confers advantage directly on its leaders and often indirectly on at least some members. Although organization is indispensable for offsetting the universal tendency toward domination, the pattern of pluralism in a particular country even while checking domination may help to sustain inequalities of various kinds, including inequality in control over the government of the state. For example, when organizations are not broadly inclusive in their membership, political inequality is a likely consequence, for, other things being equal, the organized are more influential than an equivalent number of unorganized citizens.

The inequalities to which organizational pluralism contributes would be less consequential if pluralism were invariably a dynamic force with a more or less steady thrust toward the reduction of inequalities. No theoretical reasoning I know of has ever been advanced to demonstrate that such a dynamic exists. There are grounds

* Although critics often attribute to "pluralist theory" the assertion that groups are equal in their influence over decisions, it is doubtful that anyone who might be described as a theorist of pluralism has ever made such an assertion. See appendix A.

for thinking instead that in some democratic countries, organizational pluralism develops a self-sustaining pattern over fairly long periods. In this respect, the dynamic of organizational pluralism may have rather different consequences for polyarchies than for authoritarian regimes. Because these differences in consequences may partly account for conflicting views about the values of pluralism, a brief digression may be helpful.

Like polyarchies, authoritarian regimes exist in countries with varying amounts of diversity. In some countries, notably in the Soviet Union, social and cultural diversity is enormous. Potential cleavages appear to exist along almost every kind of difference that is familiar in democratic countries: language, region, ethnic group, race, religion, status, occupation, ideology . . . An extraordinary concentration of resources in the hands of the central leadership, extremely severe sanctions against opponents, and an overwhelming (if not invariably successful) effort to eliminate all forms of organizational autonomy are necessary to prevent these differences from appearing in public conflicts. One can readily imagine that a plurality of interests and organizations would mushroom if extensive liberalization were to occur in the Soviet Union. What is true of the USSR in extreme form because of its great size and diversity holds true, though often in less extreme form, in many other countries with authoritarian regimes. Liberalization always poses a serious danger to authoritarian regimes; in some it threatens the territorial unity of the country itself.

A demand for greater personal and organizational autonomy and a lowering of the barriers to oppositions is one major point that the various internal critics of an authoritarian regime are likely to agree on—witness Sakharov, the Westernizer and liberal democrat; Solzhenitsyn, the Christian Slavophile; and Medvedev, the neo-Leninist. But because liberalization would undermine the capacity of the current rulers to dominate the government of the state, and through it much of society, it is a demand that rulers are quite likely to see, with justification, as revolutionary. Even in a comparatively liberalized hegemonic order like Yugoslavia's, a threshold exists beyond which demands for further liberalization are viewed by leaders as subversive, because any further lowering of the barriers would lead inevitably to organized political oppositions, which would threaten to undermine the dominant position of the party, its leaders, and possibly the unity of the country itself.

The situation is different in democratic countries. As a result of the comparatively low barriers to organizational autonomy, organizations tend to exist around the most salient cleavages. Given no drastic constitutional changes, if the same cleavages persist over an extended period and if the pattern of political conflict remains more or less stable, then a specific pattern of organizational pluralism may persist. The major organizations—political parties and trade unions, for example—reach the particular limits of their followings, which may be considerably short of the total numbers of hypothetically available followers but near the effective maximum set by the attitudes and expectations of organizational leaders, members, and nonmembers. Disputes become more routinized as the techniques of negotiation and conciliation are institutionalized and each antagonist grows aware of the rough limits to which the others will go. In systems of "corporate pluralism," to use Rokkan's term (Rokkan 1966, 105), the consequences of a genuine breakdown in negotiations may take on the proportions of a nearly unthinkable national disaster. The leaders in all the major organizations may conclude that a "politics of accommodation," as Lijphart has called the Dutch system (Lijphart 1975), is necessary for the very survival of the country itself.

Even in countries where the major economic organizations are less comprehensive and centralized than in the Netherlands or the Scandinavian countries, organizations involved in important conflicts often reach an accommodation with others. In practice if not in propaganda, each accepts the existence of the others and even concedes, if sometimes grudgingly, their legitimacy as spokesmen for the interests of their followers. Thereafter, none seeks seriously to destroy the others; in any case, each has enough resources to make the costs far too high. Although such a system is sometime said to be in equilibrium, it would be more accurate to say that among the major organized interests there is a mutual accommodation or détente. When this happens, organized pluralism is a stabilizing force that is highly conservative in the face of demands for innovative structural change. Each of the major organized forces in a country prevents the others from making changes that might seriously damage its perceived interests. As a consequence, structural reforms that would significantly and rapidly redistribute control, status, income, wealth, and other resources are impossible to achieve—unless, ironically, they are made at the expense of the unorganized. In this way, a powerful social force that in authoritarian countries carries with it the unmistakable odor of revolution can in democratic countries strongly reinforce the status quo.

Deforming Civic Consciousness

The possibility that organizations with a relatively high degree of autonomy, loyalty, and influence can exist within the boundaries of a state—city-state or nation-state—has always created difficulties for both political theory and political practice. Some of these difficulties, though by no means all, arise because organizational pluralism generally exists symbiotically with a plurality of interests. Where citizens or other actors can more or less freely express and advocate their interests (as they perceive them), and where organizations can be more or less freely formed, activists form and join organizations in order to advance their interests. Organizations in turn create, advance, protect, strengthen, and preserve some of the interests of some of their members. This linkage between organizational pluralism and a plurality of interests means that whatever creates the one creates the other, provided only that it is permissible to form organizations and to advocate a diversity of interests. Rousseau clearly understood the linkage between a plurality of associations and a plurality of interests. By expressing and giving strength to particular interests, associations would impede the expression of the general will. Although he was neither so naive nor so optimistic as to believe that all particular interests and associations could actually be prevented—they were too much in the natural order of things for that—in his view they could and should be severely inhibited.

Organizations, then, are not mere relay stations that receive and send signals from their members about their interests. Organizations amplify the signals and generate new ones. Often they sharpen particularistic demands at the expense of broader needs, and short-run against long-run needs. Indeed, in the struggle to influence decisions and policies, an organization that attempted to represent a broad range of its members' latent concerns would be seriously handicapped. For not only would it thereby disperse its resources over a variety of activities and thus lose the advantage of concentration, but in a country with a multiplicity of cleavages all the country's conflicts would then be mirrored within the organization itself. Leaders therefore play down potential cleavages and conflicts among their own members and exaggerate the salience of conflicts with outsiders. Organizations thereby strengthen both solidarity and division, cohesion and conflict; they reinforce solidarity among members and conflicts with nonmembers. Because associations help to fragment the concerns of citizens, interests that many citizens might share—latent ones perhaps—may be slighted.

What is more, by emphasizing aspects of the self that are enhanced by organizational or segmental gains, organizational pluralism helps to produce in political actors a set of perceptions and beliefs, even a persistent political culture, in which the absence of a common, public, or widely shared set of interests is a self-fulfilling prophecy. I and my "interests" become attached to my social segment and my organizations; leaders in my organizations in turn seek to increase the strength and salience of my attachments; my public interest becomes identical in my mind with my segmental interest; since what is true of me is true of others, we all passively or actively support the organizational fight on behalf of our particularistic interests; finally, as levels of distrust rise and effective communication declines, the "rational" pursuit by each of us of our particularistic self-interest may lead to mutually damaging outcomes.

Distorting the Public Agenda

Suppose that government officials adopt policy x rather than y or z. Although y is on the agenda it is not seriously considered, while z is not seriously considered because it is not on the agenda at all. Suppose we have good reasons for believing that if officials had seriously considered these alternatives they might have preferred one of them to x. We could then conclude that the public agenda had been distorted.

Like the notion of a deformed civic consciousness, the idea of a distorted public agenda presupposes a hypothetical alternative—an undistorted public agenda. Because both notions depend for their meaning on a counterfactual description, they run the risk of asserting nothing more convincing than one's own biases. Despite this drawback, it would be a mistake to write off the idea of a distorted public agenda as meaningless. For in some cases it is possible to furnish a convincing description of an alternative that (a) is excluded from serious consideration and (b) if it were seriously considered, would significantly alter the outcome of the decision-making process.

Consider the budgetary process in Congress until 1974. Although the president annually presents Congress with a budget document containing an overall view of expenditures and revenues, before the Budget Act of 1974 Congress considered expenditures and revenues in a highly fragmented and decentralized fashion. In each house, authorizations for the federal agencies were considered separately by various legislative committees; actual appropriations were handled by the appropriations committees, working mainly in subcommittees; and revenues were considered by yet another committee in each chamber (Ways and Means in the House, Finance in the Senate). *At no point* did either house ever consider the magnitude of total expenditures, much less the relation between total expenditures and total revenues. Total expenditures and the size of the probable surplus or deficit were unconsidered by-products of a number of detailed decisions, each influenced strongly by interest groups with the access and resources to participate effectively. Because the overall budget was at no time on the agenda of Congress, the budgetary process responded far more to the pressures of these highly organized interest groups than to considerations of the general economic consequences of federal expenditures and revenues, concerning which Congress never made a decision. Although many scholars and members of Congress judged the process to be seriously defective, until 1974 those who gained the greatest short-run benefits from the way it worked—organized interests with lobbyists in Washington, members of Congress serving on particular committees, and officials in specific executive agencies—successfully prevented change.

In much the same way, until 1934 the process of congressional decisionmaking on protective tariffs offered an open field to organized producer groups eager to gain protection for their products. As with the budget, the general tariff level was an unconsidered by-product of a large number of decentralized and uncoordinated decisions about particular tariffs, each made primarily in response to pressures from the producer groups that stood to gain the most. In both cases, then, the agenda of Congress excluded consideration of matters of signal importance—the overall level of the budget or tariffs. In both cases, there were convincing reasons for believing that a majority of members in each house and probably a majority of citizens would prefer that overall levels be considered rather than ignored. In both cases, therefore, it was reasonable to assert that the omission distorted the public agenda. In both cases, correcting the distortion required a basic change in the process of decision making. That in both cases the change was finally made shows that while processes of decision making in systems of organized pluralism are not always easy to change, they are not necessarily locked forever into place by overpowering social forces.

These examples also suggest some of the ways in which organized pluralism may help to bring about a distorted public agenda. The unequal resources that allow organizations to stabilize injustice also enable them to exercise unequal influence in determining what alternatives are seriously considered. Moreover, by reinforcing civic orientations that encourage group egoism, foster distrust of other groups, and weaken perceptions of a general interest more important than the specific concerns of each organized group, organizations encourage more serious consideration of alternatives that promise visible short-run benefits to a relatively small number of organized citizens than alternatives that promise substantial long-run benefits to a larger number of unorganized citizens.

Alienating Final Control
Critics sometimes describe organizational pluralism as a system in which private groups wrongfully appropriate public functions. The main culprits are usually identified as economic organizations—business firms, labor unions, associations of farmers, and so on. Crucial decisions on economic matters are said to be outside the effective control of the national legislature, not to mention the electorate. The United States has been so described, as have the Scandinavian systems of "corporate pluralism."

It is not difficult to show that private or nongovernmental organizations perform public functions. To show that they have *wrongfully* appropriated public functions, however, requires several normative, conceptual, and empirical judgments that are rarely made explicit. In practice, how are we to judge whther a subsystem in a democratic country has wrongfully appropriated a public function?

The question is much trickier than it looks. In making my assumptions explicit I propose to consider the question exclusively from the democratic perspective described in chapter 2. As we saw there, one criterion of democracy in its ideal meaning is final control over the agenda of the demos. Final control proscribes any irrecoverable delegation by citizens of their proper control over public matters, that is, alienation. Final control does not, however, bar delegation. The archenemy of alienation of popular sovereignty,

Rousseau, recognized that in practice even a citizen body small enough to govern itself directly by means of citizen assembly could hardly be expected to administer its own public affairs and would therefore have to delegate some decisions to officials. If citizens in a city-state must delegate, a fortiori a much larger body of citizens, such as that of a nation-state, would find it necessary to delegate. In practice, therefore, every democratic system requires delegation.

In a democratic system as large as that needed to govern a country, to what agents might citizens reasonably choose to delegate some of their collective authority over public affairs? At the outset, to their representatives. To simplify the discussion, I want to assume, *pace* the *Social Contract*, that representation does not constitute alienation in principle and, despite experience to the contrary, does not risk alienation in practice. A further simplification will also help to make a difficult argument more manageable. To avoid introducing a highly complex and variable set of relationships I would like to refer to legislature and executive collectively simply as representatives. So our question now is, To what agents might representatives in a democratic country properly delegate some of their authority? The most obvious possibilities are bureaucracies over which the representatives would retain unilateral control, courts, smaller governments under the democratic control of a local demos, and private or nonstate associations. Representatives could explicitly delegate authority to agents like these; or they could do so implicitly, simply by leaving certain matters in their hands.

Suppose now that practical or constitutional barriers prevent representatives from exercising control over important decisions made by one or more subsystems, whether bureaucracies, courts, local governments, or private organizations. Must we conclude that the demos lacks final control over the agenda of public affairs—and that to this extent the political system is undemocratic?

We must not be so hasty. The boundaries between delegations and alienation of final control over public affairs are far from clear. For one thing, even in a fully democratic system certain fundamental rights would properly lie outside the authority of the demos or its representatives. Consequently it would be a serious mistake to say that on these matters the demos has delegated its control; for a demos cannot rightfully delegate to others control over matters it does not rightfully possess itself. It would therefore be wrong to conclude that its inability to control decisions on these matters implies that it has alienated its control. For what it cannot rightfully delegate, it cannot alienate. Finally, for these reasons it would be misleading to say that on these matters private groups have wrongfully appropriated public functions.

How can we justify the conclusion that even in a fully democratic system some organizations would be entitled to a certain range of autonomy vis-à-vis the demos and its representatives? The conclusion follows from the commitment to the democratic process itself. To affirm that the democratic process is desirable is to assert that citizens must possess all the rights necessary to that process. If a body of citizens were to deprive any citizen of any fundamental right necessary to the democratic process, then by its own action it would violate the criteria of the democratic process. The question is not whether it could do so as a practical matter but whether it could rightfully do so. It could not rightfully do so because certain rights logically should be regarded as inalienable in a democratic system: to yield these rights would be inconsistent with the existence of the democratic process itself. It follows, then, that whenever the control of the citizen body is limited by the fundamental political rights of its citizens, one could not correctly describe this limitation as alienation, since these matters are not properly within the authority of the citizens to delegate in the first place.

It goes without saying that determining what constitutes fundamental political rights in a democratic order is in practice far from simple. Earlier in this chapter I argued that in a political system as large as a country, the rights required for the democratic process make political parties both necessary and possible. Obviously, this reasoning would not justify a political party's doing whatever it chooses. It does justify the conclusion, however, that in a fully democratic country the demos and its representatives could have no proper claim to a power to suppress political parties. Like political parties, in a fully democratic country many other kinds of organizations would also be entitled to a range of autonomy, not merely because a delegation of authority is contingent on the sufferance of the representatives but because a certain range of organizational autonomy is necessary to the democratic process itself. The upshot is that in order to justify an assertion about alienation of final control, or the private appropriation of public functions, one must provide a reasoned judgment—however difficult it may be—as to the kinds and range of organizational autonomy that, as a matter of fundamental political rights, should be regarded as outside the final control of representatives.

Yet surely no one would be so foolish as to insist that whatever range of autonomy any organization in any democratic country happens to possess it possesses as a matter of fundamental political right. In a fully democratic country, representatives could properly exercise control over a very broad range of organizational activities. Within this range, on purely prudential grounds the representatives could properly delegate their immediate control to others. We now return full circle: how are we to determine in practice whether representatives have retained final control over the decisions of a subsystem?

A determination of this kind evidently requires answers to three questions: (1) Is the autonomy of the subsystem a matter of fundamental political right? If not, (2) Does the subsystem make decisions that violate important policies of the representatives? If so (3) Can representatives assert sufficient control over the wayward subsystems to bring them readily into compliance?

For three reasons the answer to the last question is sometimes no. First, because subsystems invariably have access to resources of their own they can usually raise the costs of control by representatives. Their resistance to control is often facilitated by the great weight of institutionalized structures, prevailing ideology, tradition, and so on: all the powerful factors mentioned in the last chapter. Second, because of these factors, the relative advantages of some degree of decentralization, and the relative disadvantages of extreme centralization, representatives are limited in the means they can use to bring wayward systems into compliance with their policies. Often they cannot rely exclusively on legal or administrative command. Nor can they simply convert autonomous subsystems into central bureaucratic agencies (which in many cases are also notoriously difficult for representatives to control). To obtain compliance, representatives are often compelled to offer costly inducements to important subsystems—which in turn provide the subsystems with resources for resistance. Lindblom has described "the list of necessary inducements" that protect "the privileged position of businessmen" as "whatever businessmen need as a condition for performing the tasks that fall to them in a market system: income and wealth, deference, prestige, influence, power, and authority, among others" (Lindblom 1977, 174). Other organizations are also, in this sense, in a privileged position, though their privileges may be considerably less than those of businessmen. In Britain, for example, Labour and Conservative governments alike have often found it impossible to carry out their economic policies because trade unions reject the limits on wage increases the government's policies require, and no government can compel their compliance. In the Scandinavian countries, the control of representatives over national economic policy is severely limited by whatever the heads of the labor unions and employers' associations agree to in their annual negotiations. In the Scandinavian systems of "corporate pluralism," economic decisions of crucial importance to the country have in effect been turned over to organizations that, for all practical purposes, the government cannot control—a fact made dramatically visible in Sweden during the nationwide strikes and lockouts of 1980, after the annual negotiations between the employers' association and the labor organization broke down.

A third factor makes it impossible for representatives in a democratic country to bring recalcitrant organizations into compliance: the sheer complexity of organized pluralism. Indeed, nowadays national policy is often based on this assumption. Representatives readily yield some of their control, knowing that should they attempt to impose a national policy on complex subsystems they would produce chaos.

Although complexity has itself proved to be a complex concept, we can capture enough meaning for the discussion here by saying that complexity increases with an increase in the variety and number of relatively independent subsystems and with an increase in the extent of variation in the possible relations between the subsystems. As complexity increases in a centrally controlled system, those in charge of steering need more and more information to avoid disaster, let alone arrive close to their chosen destination. Yet in modern democratic countries the complexity of the patterns, processes, and activities of a large number of relatively autonomous organizations has outstripped theory, existing information, the capacity of the system to transmit such information as exists, and the ability of representatives—or others, for that matter—to comprehend it. An illuminating insight is provided by Gary Brewer's experiment with a computer model of a national economy (Brewer 1975).

Brewer constructed "a simple computer model of a fictitious national system" in which gross national product at time t is a function of consumption, investment, and government expenditures. He then increased the complexity of the model by incrementally adding ten changes, such as disaggregating the national system into ten spatial sectors, introducing population subsystems, providing for migration between spatial sectors, and introducing various random disturbances. At the tenth time period, on one set of assumptions, there were 2,770 internal structural links in the model. "One simple change has approximately *doubled* the number of structural links in the model and has considerably increased the degree of complexity" (191). He comments: "If our simple analysis is indicative, understanding a formal symbolic model, the theoretical image it replicates, and the context purportedly described by model and image, declines rapidly as size increases. One loses control. Confidence in the symbol system's structure decreases as the number of elements, their interconnections, their relationships, and error in measurement increase. The central point is essentially this: At some level of size for a given model we decidedly lose the ability to make structural revisions, i.e., to improve the model theoretically" (199).

If for these three reasons representatives in modern democratic countries find it extremely difficult and at times impossible to assert sufficient control over wayward subsystems to bring them under control, then are we not entitled to say that they—and the demos—have lost final control over the agenda of public affairs?

*   *   *   *   *

In introducing the four defects that I have just described, I said that organizational pluralism is "implicated" in these difficulties. Thus I chose a word that allows for great ambiguity as to causes. Can we reasonably charge organizational pluralism in democratic countries with *causing* these problems, or at the very least constituting a significant causal factor? Or is the charge the very different one that the existence of organizational pluralism is not sufficient to remedy these defects and might even inhibit solutions?

Two procedures can be used in the best circumstances to provide conclusive answers to questions like these: controlled experiments and quasi-experimental statistical methods. For obvious reasons, neither of these can be used to provide satisfactory answers to our questions. We must follow instead the more usual process of working our way through the available evidence, substituting thought experiments for real ones and qualitative for quantitative data. In pursuing this process, however, it is helpful to isolate some of the crucial factors that may be "implicated" in the problem of democratic pluralism.

1. To what extent are the defects I have described characteristic of democratic pluralism as such, and to what extent are they peculiar to specific countries, such as the United States? In recent years much description and criticism of pluralism (often with meanings attributed to the term different from the meaning I intend here) has

been written by American political scientists who explicitly or implicitly focus on American experience.* Yet there are good reasons for thinking that patterns of organizational pluralism vary a great deal in different democratic countries. In the next chapter, therefore, I want to examine some of these variations.

2. To what extent are the defects a result of the fact that polyarchy is an incomplete realization of democratic ideals? The defects of democratic pluralism might be less a consequence of failures in pluralism as such than of failures in democratization. Conversely, does the attempt to apply the democratic process on a large scale necessarily impose limits on all remedies, in the sense that all remedies are bound to suffer from grave disadvantages? In chapter 5 I want to consider whether the defects of democratic pluralism might be cured by a more democratic pluralism.

3. To what extent are the defects a consequence of the fact that polyarchy exists only in countries with privately owned, market-oriented economies? In other words, are the defects a consequence more of the structures of capitalism than of pluralism or polyarchy? To explore these questions, in chapter 6 I shall consider whether the defects might be remedied by structural changes in the economic order involving radically more centralized government control over economic decisions, or radically more decentralization, or (accompanying either of these) a radical shift from private to public ownership of large enterprises.

4. To what extent are the defects primarily a result of a civic consciousness that stresses egoism rather than altruism or benevolence? And to what extent are these civic orientations a result of a capitalist society and thus perhaps remediable in a different economic order? Conversely, to what extent is egoism more the result of the scale of modern society and independent economic structures as such? These questions will be explored in chapter 7.

---

*These include Bachrach and Baratz (1962), Connolly (1969), Kariel (1961), McConnell (1966), Lowi (1969), and Lindblom (1977, 1979) [see, however, Lindblom (1965) and Braybrooke and Lindblom (1963)]. A number of the deficiencies of pluralism described in this chapter have been emphasized by these writers.

4

National Variations

Just as it would be wrong to think that every country manifesting organizational pluralism is necessarily democratic, so it would be wrong to suppose that all democratic countries display pretty much the same constellation of independent organizations. The constellation of pluralism in democratic countries appears to be a result of at least five major structural features. Of these, two are common to all democratic countries. By definition, all democratic countries are governed by polyarchal regimes; in the last chapter I showed how the political institutions of polyarchy make relatively independent organizations both necessary and inevitable. It is also true, though in this case empirically and not by definition, that the economic order in all democratic countries has historically been capitalist, in the sense that firms are in the main privately owned and market oriented. In the next chapter I want to consider whether democratic pluralism is inextricably bound up with capitalism or might also exist in a country with a socialist economy.

The two common factors can hardly explain variations in the constellation of organizational pluralism in different countries. To account for variations we must look to features that vary from one democratic country to another. Three such structural features are patterns of conflict and cleavage, concrete political institutions, and the inclusiveness and concentration of organizations.

How variations in these three structural features could themselves be explained would require a comparative study of the history of every democratic country. As Stein Rokkan often pointed out, contemporary European party systems reflect past conflicts and social cleavages more than current ones. To explain European party systems, he showed, one must go back to the Reformation, or earlier. In what follows, however, I shall focus on the three major kinds of structural variations as explanations but make no effort to account for them.

Conflicts and Cleavages

The issues involved in conflicts between members of the various social aggregates in a country may touch upon virtually any aspect of life. Of particular interest to us, however, are conflicts that bring into question the conduct or structure of the government of the state. The most crucial issues in such conflicts may lie elsewhere—in economic relationships, for example, or in religious or linguistic cleavages. But in democratic countries, conflicts in economic, social, and cultural spheres are likely to spill over into disputes about the government of the state—its personnel, conduct, policies, structure, legitimacy, and so on. For the sake of convenience, I am going to call conflicts that involve the government of the state *political conflicts*.

   Political conflicts form patterns of such bewildering variety as to defy a concise summary. Consider some questions that a full description of a country's pattern of political conflicts might reasonably be expected to answer:

To what extent are the principal actors involved in political conflicts, organizations or unorganized aggregates rather than individuals?

How many collective adversaries are ordinarily involved in political conflicts—two, three, four, more?

Do the characteristics of the allies and adversaries change in a significant way from one political conflict to another, or do they remain pretty much the same?

As a consequence, do the same actors tend always to be allies and adversaries, or are allies in one conflict often adversaries in another?

How strong or intense is the antagonism between the contestants? Do they see one another as enemies locked in a struggle for survival, or at the other extreme as friends, neighbors, or fellow citizens who have a temporary disagreement?

Finally, if a pattern can be described at all, how enduring is it? Does one pattern characterize political life for only a few years, or does it persist much longer, perhaps for a generation or more? Is there an oscillation from one pattern to another, so that the oscillation itself forms a more inclusive pattern of political conflicts?

Because a matrix of possible answers would be not only of appalling complexity but far beyond the reach of data and theory, figure 1 offers a highly simplified scheme. To make the meaning of these eight patterns a bit more concrete, let me also show them in a slightly different way in table 1. The symbols a_1, b_3, and so on can stand either for individual persons or for some shared characteristic of the individuals, such as working class, middle class, Protestant, Francophone, Black, and so on. When these shared characteristics are all elements in a more inclusive category of analysis, such as class, religion, language, or race, the inclusive category is often referred to as a political *cleavage*. Thus, if the adversaries in a bipolar conflict consist mainly of Protestants on one side and Catholics on the other, as in Northern Ireland, then religion constitutes a political cleavage. When conflicts reinforce one another, the composition of the adversaries remains essentially the same from one conflict to another: the individuals or the shared characteristics that form the cleavages do not change. One's allies today are one's allies tomorrow; one's opponents today are one's opponents tomorrow. With crosscutting cleavages, on the other hand, one's allies today will probably be one's opponents in the near future.

None of the eight theoretical possibilities is empirically absurd, though this is sometimes thought to be the case. For example, it is often supposed, particularly by Marxists, that reinforcing conflicts must be bipolar; if reinforcing conflicts were always bipolar, then the segmented conflicts in patterns v and vi would never exist. Yet in the Netherlands from the First World War until fairly recently,

FIGURE 1. Some Patterns of Political Conflict

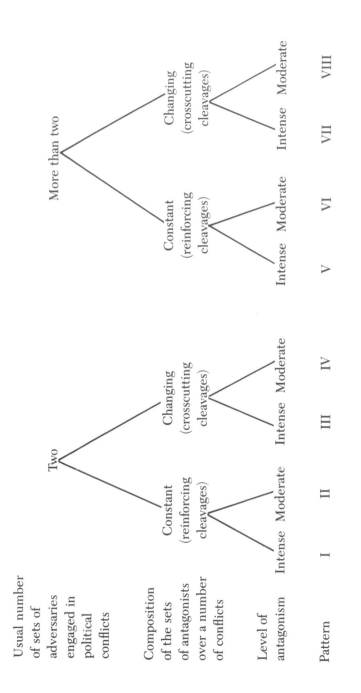

TABLE 1. Some Patterns of Political Conflict

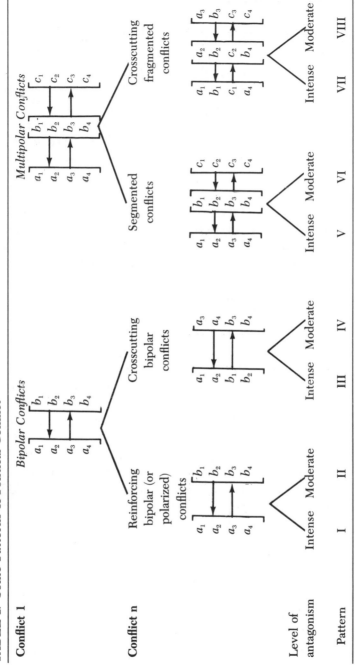

political conflict occurred mainly among four groups: Catholics, orthodox Calvinists, Labor, and Liberals. For most Catholics and most orthodox Calvinists, religion was the principal cleavage in political life—indeed in practically all organized aspects of life; those who were neither Catholic nor orthodox Calvinist were divided by social class, which thus constituted the main cleavage between Labor and Liberals. Again, it was pretty nearly an article of faith among political scientists and sociologists for some years, especially in the United States, that democratic governments could not survive unless the main cleavages were crosscutting. It was supposed that whereas crosscutting cleavages would moderate the intensity of conflict and thereby encourage compromise, reinforcing cleavages would surely produce such intense conflicts as to make compromise difficult or impossible. Reinforcing conflicts would therefore lead to the intense antagonisms and conflicts of patterns I and V, rather than to the moderation of patterns II and VI. Crosscutting cleavages, on the other hand, would produce the moderation in political conflicts found in patterns IV and VIII, rather than the intense antagonism found in III and VII.

On this understanding of political life, four patterns would be unlikely to exist at all in democratic countries: patterns of moderate conflict stemming from reinforcing cleavages (II and VI) and patterns of intense conflict resulting from crosscutting cleavages (III and VII). Although the highly conflictive patterns I and V might well occur, if they persisted they would produce such profound instability that a country would be unable to maintain democratic institutions. Consequently, in relatively stable democratic countries one would find only the two remaining patterns, IV and VIII, in both of which crosscutting cleavages produce moderate rather than severe conflicts. This interpretation is no longer tenable, however, because democratic institutions have endured for a generation or more in several countries with distinctive subcultures and a pattern of persistently segmented conflicts, particularly the Netherlands and Belgium.

Another common belief is that in a capitalist country two highly antagonistic classes are sure to develop and sooner or later political life will reflect the fundamental conflict between these two classes. Since this view is often said to falsify the major premise advanced in chapter 2 and in other ways plays an important part in some of the controversies over pluralism, it is important to examine it carefully.

Classes and Polarization

How best to conceive of classes has been at the forefront of the problems and controversies of social theorists ever since Marx, and the matter is still far from settled. In whatever fashion class is defined, it usually shows up as a significant cleavage in political conflicts. In many countries, class accounts more than any other cleavage for the support voters give to different parties, though the relative importance of class in voting and party support varies a great deal from one advanced country to another and even in the same country over rather brief periods of time. It is an easy step from the persistence of class to the view that political life must reflect a persistent conflict between two classes. Although the idea of society as essentially divided into two main classes is by no means Marxist or modern, it is the authority of Marx, and the importance of Marxist ideas in the contemporary world, that give intellectual standing to the idea today. Whether Marx actually presented or intended to present a scenario in which the two antagonistic classes in his historical drama were driven by their objective conditions to a polarized conflict of rising intensity is a much debated question that I have no intention of entering into here. Whatever Marx intended, many Marxists have held that in any system of industrial capitalism the system of classes must be essentially dichotomous, consisting of bourgeoisie and proletariat; between these two classes there is an inherent conflict of fundamental interests; this conflict of fundamental interests will tend to generate intense polarized conflicts between the two classes; and this polarization will manifest itself in conflicts over the policies, personnel, conduct, class composition, and structure of the government of the state, that is, in overt political conflict. While they may not share the apocalyptic aspects of this vision, many non-Marxists also believe that political life is for the most part a struggle between two classes, groups, or strata—the haves and have-nots, business and labor, corporate enterprise and the public, and so on.

However, the scenario of class polarization has nowhere been played out, at least in democratic countries.* Intense polarized conflict—pattern I—does seem to occur occasionally, though not necessarily along the cleavage line of social status or economic class. As in the Marxist scenario suggested above, intense polarization is unstable, though for different reasons. Either the political elites, fearing the consequences of polarization, find solutions to the conflict that both attenuate the antagonisms and encourage a different pattern of conflict to emerge as in Austria under the system of *Proporz* after World War II; or else, as in Chile, an authoritarian regime is inaugurated that suppresses its opponents and destroys democratic institutions. However, to explain why intense polarization is unstable does not account for the infrequent appearance even of moderate bipolarity in democratic countries. Moderate polarization such as exists in New Zealand is hardly a source of instability for a regime. How then can we account for the fact that even moderate polarization (pattern II) is comparatively uncommon, at least as a persistent and overarching pattern of political conflict?

As Joseph LaPalombara's analysis (1974) of comparative evidence indicates, and as others have also found, in most democratic countries several different cleavages exist, and the intersection of these cleavages produces crosscutting or segmented patterns rather than polarization. That crosscutting and segmentation are more common than polarization also helps to account for the fact that where class polarization has appeared it has been moderate rather than severe. For class polarization tends to exist only in a few homogeneous countries like New Zealand and Sweden where cleavages formed around language, religion, race, ethnic group, region, and so on are not salient enough to disturb the effects of differences in social class. Class polarization mainly occurs, then, in culturally

*Citations to evidence on this point will be found in appendix B.

homogeneous countries. But precisely because these countries are highly homogeneous, they generally manage to deal with their conflicts rather easily. Consequently, even where class polarization has appeared, it has generally led to a pattern of moderate conflict within a rather consensual political environment.

To account more fully for the fact that extreme political polarization along the cleavage line of class has rarely appeared in democratic countries would call for a deeper and more extensive explanation than I have given here. To anticipate an account more fully fleshed out in chapter 7, one might conjecture that concrete human experiences, together with the cognitive and affective capacities that humanity has so far manifested, provide too weak and narrow a base for creating a strong sense of solidarity among persons and groups outside the small, specific, and idiosyncratic cluster of people with whom each of us is most intimately associated during the most crucial periods of our lives. Solidarity with abstract entities like "working class," "nation," "the church," and so on are unlikely to arise spontaneously through everyday experiences; they require a heavy investment in more or less deliberate socialization and indoctrination. Typically, family and school make a huge investment in the child's acquisition of the mother tongue, which then becomes a lasting part of one's identity. For similar reasons, religion, ethnic group, and, in racially diverse countries, race gain an early advantage. It takes no stretching of human capacities to acquire rather early in life some solidarity with one's social peers. In addition, political elites usually see to it that indoctrination in loyalty to the more abstract entities of nationality and country begins early and lasts late. Though class may be related in various ways to some of these factors, it must nonetheless compete with them. Over against such relatively deep and even nonrational attachments, the sense of solidarity with others who may occupy similar but distant economic positions necessarily arrives comparatively late, if at all, in a person's development and is less dependent on emotional ties arising out of direct contacts than on the abstract reasoning required to weave a network of common interest between oneself and remote others. Although few abstract concepts have more strongly influenced modern social theory and ideology than the notion of class, in advanced countries the theoretical concept is rarely transformed into an actual consciousness of class solidarity strong enough to overcome the effects of other attachments, more primordial and often more parochial, formed out of the experiences of daily life.

To be sure, one can interpret cleavages other than those formed by social class as crumbling obstacles to class consciousness, left behind by the slow recession of traditional society and early capitalism, destined nevertheless to erode under the glacial push of new economic relationships. However, this interpretation underestimates the continuing strength of primordial identifications formed by subcultures centered on religion, region, ethnic group, race, and language, and of new identifications centered on a variety of social and economic differences that do not fall nicely along a single prominent cleavage line but generate several cleavages, like those that tend to divide skilled from unskilled workers, blue collar from white collar, service workers from professionals, and so on. In addition, ideological diversity, especially among elites, often contributes to crosscutting and segmented patterns. In fact a standard element in the history of all working-class movements is the intensity of the ideological cleavages among the very leaders most engaged in trying to increase the class consciousness and solidarity of the workers.

Because of the crosscutting or segmentation produced by these various cleavages, most democratic countries have managed to pass through the critical period of early industrialization without deep class polarization. Because of the persistence of older (and, to many Marxists, anachronistic) sources of cleavage, a solidary working class has nowhere lined up against a solidary bourgeoisie. In time, cross-class political parties have developed that exploit some of the older cleavages and solidarities, particularly religion, and play down class animosities. Meanwhile, blue-collar workers have leveled off or declined as a percentage of the working force. In later stages of economic change, growing employment in tertiary sectors has created new crosscutting cleavages. Political perspectives become increasingly independent of occupation and other objective factors. In postindustrial countries, if intense polarization occurs at all, it is more likely to reflect cleavages resulting from conflicting ideas and ideologies that are not strongly related to such time-honored categories of explanation as occupation, social status, and income.

The evidence and the argument should not be overinterpreted. As I have already said, class is not unimportant in political conflict. The point is, however, that in most democratic countries social class is only an element, albeit a significant one, in a pattern of political conflict that is rarely polarized. What is more, in democratic countries where political conflict *is* persistently polarized, the consequence is usually moderate rather than intense conflict.

Political Institutions

The concrete political institutions of a country also cause variations in the morphology of democratic pluralism. Although political institutions themselves are partly shaped by a country's cleavages and conflicts, once political arrangements become institutionalized they acquire a force of their own. Indeed in some countries—Britain, the Scandinavian countries, Switzerland, and the United States, for example—many of the most crucial constitutional features antedate industrialization and are partly the consequence of older rather than contemporary patterns of cleavage and conflict.

Variations in three kinds of political institutions are particularly important. Constitutional norms, and the practices influenced by these norms, vary in the extent to which authority is partitioned among and within such major institutions as executive, legislature, bureaucracy, and judiciary as well as such territorial structures as cantons, provinces, states, and the like. At the one extreme, in countries like Switzerland and the United States, constitutional norms provide for an extensive division of authority by means of both federalism and separation of powers. As a result, the government of the state is itself fragmented into a number of separate subsystems, each possessing a good deal of autonomy in relation to the others. At the other extreme, in countries like New Zealand and Britain, a unitary rather than a federal system, combined with parliamentary government rather than a strict separation of powers between executive and legislature, make for considerably greater concentration of constitutional authority.

Second, electoral and party systems vary all the way from New Zealand, where two comparatively centralized parties are for all practical purposes the sole competitors in national elections, to the Netherlands and Israel, where a dozen parties may gain some representation and none approaches a majority. Once again, electoral and party systems are not independent of the other factors that have been mentioned—patterns of cleavage and conflict and the constitutional norms themselves. Yet these factors do not wholly explain the extraordinary variation in party systems in polyarchies, or the reciprocal effects of electoral arrangements and party systems on cleavages, political conflicts, consensus, and coalition building, or the relative influence of majorities and minorities on the conduct of government.

A third set of political institutions that vary widely among polyarchies has to do with the participation and influence of interest organizations over key political decisions. In general, regular institutionalized participation by interest organizations is probably most extensive for certain kinds of decisions that bear strategically on economic performance: wages, prices, working conditions, location, investment, and so on. In several countries—Germany, Norway, Sweden, and The Netherlands—the major interest organizations play central roles. Thus Rokkan wrote of Norway:

The extension of the franchise to all adults and the maintenance of a strict majoritarian rule of decision-making in the legislature made it possible for a movement of the hitherto underprivileged to rise to power. But the parallel growth of a vast network of interest organizations and other corporate bodies made it impossible to rule by any simple "50 percent plus" principle. To understand the strategies and counterstrategies of government and opposition we have to analyze the bargaining processes between the giant alliances of such associations and corporations. The vote potential constitutes only one among many different power resources brought to bear in these bargaining processes: what really counts is the capacity to hurt or to halt a system of highly interdependent activities. . . . The crucial decisions on economic policy are rarely taken in the parties or in Parliament: the central area is the bargaining table where the government authorities meet directly with the trade union leaders, the representatives of the farmers, the small-holders, and the fishermen, and the delegates of the Employers' Association. These yearly rounds of negotiations have in fact come to mean more in the lives of rank-and-file citizens than the formal elections. In these processes of intensive interaction, the parliamentary notions of one member, one vote and majority rule make little sense. Decisions are not made through the counting of heads but through complex considerations of short-term or long-term advantages in alternative lines of compromise (Rokkan 1966, 106–07).

In other countries, particularly the United States, no such institutionalized process exists. The participation and influence of interest organizations is more fragmented, decentralized, and indirect.

Inclusiveness and Concentration of Organizations

The morphology of pluralism in a specific country also depends on the inclusiveness and concentration of organizations. On the one hand, countries vary a great deal in the proportion of the population included in organizations. In twelve polyarchies for which satisfactory data are available, the proportion of persons not members of any voluntary association varies from 20 percent in Sweden to 70 percent in Italy; the median is 40 percent. The proportion of the population in organizations is highest in the Scandinavian countries; aside from Italy, it is lowest in the United Kingdom and West Germany (Pestoff 1977, 65 and 168). Membership in economic organizations—trade unions, producer co-ops and professional associations—ranges from 51 percent of the population in Sweden to about 16 percent in Italy and 17–18 percent in West Germany. Membership in noneconomic associations varies from 62 percent in the United States to 18 percent in Italy and 21 percent in West Germany. As the figures for West Germany, Sweden, the United States, and Britain indicate, variations in organizational membership are great even in the advanced industrial countries.

In addition, there are significant variations in the extent to which organizations are concentrated in peak associations whose leaders are able to negotiate and enter into decisions in behalf of the members of the entire coalition. In the Scandinavian countries, there is a single trade-union movement; in France, two; in Italy, three. In the United States, some of the largest and most influential trade unions are outside the AFL-CIO, which itself is highly decentralized. In Britain, the trade unions are even more numerous and decentralized than in the United States. The Scandinavian system of "corporate pluralism," to use Rokkan's phrase, is made possible by, and in turn probably reinforces, the authority of the top trade-union leaders in negotiating the annual decisions. In the United States, such negotiations would require nothing less than an immense parliament of trade-union leaders.

Consequences

One might reasonably wonder whether these variations have important consequences. To see the consequences more clearly, consider a country in which conflicts among organized interests occur on important economic issues: wages, prices, unemployment, inflation, productivity, and so on. Suppose, however, that the actors involved are not highly antagonistic, in part perhaps because of cross-cutting cleavages; the conflicts are rather moderate; and negotiations pretty readily lead to settlements that the participants regard as reasonable. Suppose further that the country is unitary, not federal, and ordinarily has a relatively unified cabinet with steady support for its policies in parliament. The government itself participates in the negotiations and can expect parliament to support what it agrees to. Finally, assume that the interest organizations are both highly centralized in structure and highly inclusive in membership (*i* in table 2).

TABLE 2. Structure and Membership of Organizations

	Highly centralized organizations	Moderately or highly decentralized organizations
Highly inclusive membership	i	ii
Moderately or weakly inclusive (exclusive) membership	iii	iv

Each of the major functional aggregates—labor, business, farmers, consumers—is organized in a single association with top leaders of very considerable influence over the decisions of the association. It is easy to see that these characteristics of our hypothetical country would encourage the development of centralized bargaining at the national level among the top leaders of the key associations. The practice of centralized national bargaining—Rokkan's corporate pluralism—has thus become institutionalized, let us say, and is now a basic part of the country's concrete political institutions and practices. Our hypothetical country, then, looks something like Sweden, Norway, and Denmark.

What are the likely consequences of a system of centralized national bargaining or corporate pluralism? I want to single out two sets of consequences: for the location of direct power and for the convergence of interests.

As for the location of power, in their negotiations the functional associations become a kind of parliament, which, as Rokkan pointed out, effectively displaces the regular parliament on certain key questions. In this sense, a system of centralized national bargaining comes closer than anything that has hitherto existed to the functional parliament or parliament of industry that guild socialists and others have proposed. The solution even manages to detour around a problem that such schemes have never satisfactorily solved: how to *design* a functional parliament from scratch that is both significantly different from a conventional legislature in the concerns it represents, and at the same time honors the principle of individual equality in voting. As Rokkan's comments make clear, corporate pluralism does not solve this problem; it merely manifests the problem. However, insofar as the associations and the interests they purport to represent are generally accepted by citizens as legitimate, an inherent difficulty that could cause a constitutional convention to founder is simply bypassed.

The enormous direct power the interests associations exercise through centralized national bargaining is reflected not only in their displacement of parliament. The fact is, and it is a fact likely to be widely known in the country, that the future of the economy is in the short run at least directly dependent on the outcome of the decisions made in this informal functional parliament. This is why the agreement reached is often described as a "social compact." By failing to agree on a social compact, however, labor, business, and possibly farmers, could directly bring about grave consequences. If, as the price of their agreement, the leaders of one of the associations can extort concessions to their goals without consideration for the others or for long-run effects, then any one of the associations is in a position to coerce the whole country. By their concerted action, certainly, the associations could exploit the nation.

An overly simple Hobbesian forecast would assume extortion as inevitable. But a more complex analysis, even one inspired by Hobbes, would note that the leaders engaged in centralized national bargaining are also pressed by strong incentives to avoid these harmful consequences and to achieve a reasonably fair social compact. For among the members of the associations, goals are bound to be highly interdependent: one association cannot do grave harm to the others without harming its own members. The obvious power of the associations to do great, direct, palpable harm is sobering. Thus, although the labor association might willingly accept greater inflation for less unemployment than the other associations, workers can also suffer harm as consumers and pensioners. Furthermore, if rising costs put the country's products at a competitive disadvantage in world trade, some of the consequences will bear heavily on workers. Moreover, because the organizations are inclusive, solutions that are mutually beneficial to the associations directly involved in centralized national bargaining are not likely to be harmful to any substantial body of citizens. Or to put it the other way round, an outcome that is harmful to a substantial body of citizens is bound to hurt the members of one or more of the associations, and cannot therefore be mutually beneficial. Thus *a system of centralized national bargaining can help to create a tendency toward convergence of functional or particular interests and more general interests*, and therefore toward agreement on a social compact that is in the general interest.

Despite its clear advantages, centralized national bargaining also has some dangers. The consequences for the country could be devastating if, for whatever reason, the participants become sharply polarized, cleavages tend to occur along a single fault line, antagonism intensifies, the now bipolar conflicts grow increasingly severe, and a social compact is impossible. To be sure, the system is to some extent self-correcting: foreseeing the obvious consequences of a breakdown in negotiations (or actually experiencing the effects) strengthens the incentives of antagonists to moderate their demands and search more vigorously for mutually acceptable solutions. Yet nothing in a system of centralized national bargaining ensures that mutually acceptable solutions exist or, what amounts to the same thing, can be discovered. In times of low or negative economic growth and growing deficits in foreign trade, prospects begin to look zero-sum, and negotiations may break down without agreement. They did so in Sweden in 1980, and the nationwide strike and lockout that ensued sent a wave of premonitory fear through the other Scandinavian countries.

Countries that do not have such systems of centralized national bargaining may escape these dangers, only to incur other risks.

Schematically, a country might diverge from this system in one of three ways: within the functional groups, control might be decentralized to many independent organizations as with *ii* in table 2; or the organizations might include only a small proportion of the total workforce, as with *iii*; or both might be the case, as with *iv*. Some of the consequences of a system in which control within functional groups is decentralized may be observed in Britain and the United States, where organized labor is separated into a large number of relatively independent unions (Edelstein and Warner 1976, 26). Although nationwide settlements of trade-union disputes are more common in Britain than in the United States, in both countries labor negotiations are ordinarily carried on by unions and employers in particular industries or firms. Indeed, in both countries wildcat strikes and shop steward influence have led to a further de facto decentralization. It is true that government officials may become deeply involved in attempts to reach industrywide settlements, as in the obvious case of the coal industry. Yet because control is decentralized to a number of independent unions, firms, and employers' associations, a system of centralized national bargaining has never developed in either country.

As a consequence, no functional parliament exists to make key economic decisions. In this respect the displacement of executive and legislature is less—and is certainly less obvious. Ordinarily, too, a single association has less direct power over the economy as a whole, less capacity for extortion. On the other hand, whenever the associations are centralized enough to permit industrywide bargaining in industries acutely critical for the economy as a whole, their direct power can be considerable. Again, the obvious example is coal mining in a country dependent on coal for its energy, as in Britain. In these cases, the capacity of executive and legislature to exercise direct control over economic decisions of critical importance is severely weakened.

Even more important, the incentives of the negotiators to consider general as against particular interests are weak. To the extent that each union and each employers' association is only one pair among a great many independent organizations, the consequences of each negotiation are more likely to be seen by the participants as independent of the consequences of other negotiations. In any case, the negotiators are responsive to and generally feel responsible only to people within their own organization. Union leaders or employers' representatives who sought to defend "the national interest" at the expense of the people in their own organizations would quickly lose support—and office. Thus the negotiators have little reason to consider consequences for others; they are indifferent to externalities. Yet the joint consequences of various settlements independently arrived at may have profound indirect consequences for the economy as a whole. Even if most workers and employers are organized, then, decentralized bargaining strengthens incentives to advance particular interests and weakens incentives to advance more general interests. If the direct power of the associations is less than in a system of centralized national bargaining, so also is their concern for the effects on other citizens.

If many people are not even included in the various functional associations, then the number of citizens whose interests the negotiators are likely to ignore is even larger, and to this extent the divergence between particular and general interests is likely to be even greater. It is hard to say which would have the most adverse consequences for citizens outside the particular associations engaged in bargaining: highly centralized but exclusive associations or inclusive but decentralized associations. Highly centralized associations might institute a kind of centralized national bargaining that would constitute in effect a parliament of industry that excluded much of the work force: a contemporary version of an eighteenth-century parliament based on a limited franchise and rotten boroughs. Conversely, if the functional associations are more decentralized, they will have less direct power over the economy; but in their bargaining the leaders will be concerned with the interests of only a small proportion of citizens.

Although functional economic associations furnish the clearest illustrations, the argument can be generalized. The Dutch system described by Hans Daalder (1966) and Arend Lijphart (1975), which Lijphart has called *consociational democracy*, is roughly equivalent to centralized national bargaining, but the range of issues covered is broader. The system initially grew out of a national conflict over the schools that was exacerbated into a crisis by the inability of spokesmen for the segmented subcultures to agree. Once formed, the system served for managing national conflicts over a wide range of issues. Because mutual vetoes prevented decisions thought harmful by leaders of any of the subcultures and because most of the Dutch were included in one or another of the subcultures, the system provided strong incentives to search for solutions that would be widely acceptable to most citizens. It is arguable, then, that decisions tended to converge toward a social compact that was in the general interest.

If Dutch consociational democracy might be taken as an instance of *i* in table 2, over a broad range of political decisions the United States looks to be an example of *iv*. Organizations involved in political conflicts tend not to be highly inclusive; even the trade-union movement covers only 20 percent of the labor force. Structurally, there is little centralization; political, economic, social, and cultural life is dotted with autonomous organizations. Leaders of associations therefore have strong incentives to foster the particularistic interests and demands of their own members and little incentive—indeed a strong disincentive—to exercise their influence in behalf of the interests and demands of nonmembers. Compromise is highly prized in American politics and in the society generally. But, as has been pointed out many times, there can be no assurance that the demands, goals, or interests of a majority of citizens, or even the greater number, will coincide with the outcome of compromise reached by leaders of independent organizations, none of which is very inclusive in its membership and each of which is concerned with advancing only some of the interests of some or even all of the members. The fact that associational life in the United States is both decentralized and exclusive may help to explain why the country where the advantages of pluralism have been most often celebrated also provides its severest critics.

Variations in the Problem

A great deal more systematic knowledge of variations in the constellations of pluralism is needed than is now available. Yet the account given here, though brief and incomplete, is sufficient to reveal how mistaken it is to attribute to democratic pluralism in general the characteristics of pluralism in one country, as American writers have been prone to do in taking the United States as their point of departure.

Our account justifies the conclusion that different democratic countries vary a great deal not only in the structure and processes of organizational pluralism but also in the shape and importance of the problem of democratic pluralism itself. For example, inequalities differ in kind, in degree, and in their stability. To what extent can we attribute stable inequality to democratic pluralism as such, and how much is it a consequence of the specific features of a particular country? Although, given the present state of knowledge, an answer must be imprecise, the description of stable inequality given in the last chapter fits the United States more closely than it does many other democratic countries, which should not be surprising since that description is drawn mainly from the writings of Americans. Even applied to the United States, however, the indictment of organizational pluralism as a cause of stable inequality fails to take adequately into account the extensive changes that have taken place since the 1950s in the most oppressive and most stable system of racial discrimination and political exclusion that has ever existed in any democratic country. Moreover, an analysis of American racial inequalities in a comparative context would have to account, at a minimum, for great differences among countries with federal constitutions and strong subcultural differences, such as Canada, Switzerland, and the United States.

What limits on the possibility of reducing inequalities are set, then, by democratic pluralism as such? In speculating about the answer, it is revealing to consider the experiences of countries like Sweden and Denmark with unitary constitutions where the population is relatively homogeneous culturally and where, because subcultural differences are much less pronounced (which is not to say that they are utterly insignificant), cleavages, conflicts, and inequalities coincide much less with the axes of race, religion, or language and much more with social class. In these countries, as democratization and the influence of modern ideologies undermined the historic justifications for class privileges and the constitutional means of defending them, labor and socialist parties advocating redistribution of social privileges, notably education and income, gained electoral support, particularly among working-class citizens. In a country with a unitary constitution, unified political parties, and parliamentary government, once such a party (or a coalition of parties) won a parliamentary majority, it was in a position to use the powers of the central government to carry out its redistribution policies. It would be false to contend that the constellation of democratic pluralism in these countries has perpetuated historical patterns of economic and social inequality and injustice. Instead, after decades of reform the crucial limit on redistribution has finally come to be set by the interaction of polyarchy and capitalism—that is, by how much redistribution a majority of voters will support or tolerate, on the one hand, and, on the other, the effects of redistribution on incentives in a privately owned, market-oriented economy. Once this limit has been reached, further redistribution requires structural changes in the ownership and control of the economic order itself. Partly in recognition of this new limit on redistribution, the trade-union movement and Social Democratic parties in both Denmark and Sweden in the 1970s developed new (though quite different) proposals for transferring corporate ownership to employees.

So, too, different forms of civic consciousness appear to be associated both as cause and effect with different constellations of organizational pluralism. In some countries national bargaining by inclusive organizations not only provides the peak economic associations with an opportunity to wreak immediate and disastrous damage to the country's economy, but it also makes that possibility so visible that simply in order to avoid harming their own members, the associations are strongly motivated to search for mutually satisfactory solutions to their conflicts. As a consequence, the antagonists' salient interests are not inherently inconsistent with their perceiving a broader common interest in a "social compact" which insures a fair sharing of the fruits of economic growth. At the same time, however, an inclusive system of national bargaining does not by itself guarantee that a mutually satisfactory solution actually exists. As in the prisoners' dilemma, the prevailing structure of "the game" may prevent the existence and discovery of any mutually satisfactory solution.* By contrast, more decentralized and less inclusive bargaining systems limit the amount of direct harm the antagonists can inflict on a country. But by the same token, the organizations have less reason to consider the effects of their actions on others and may be able, at least in the short run, to displace the costs to others who do not participate in the bargaining process. In these countries, then, pluralism encourages the growth of organizational egoism at public expense.

These observations indicate that, like social structures generally, organizational pluralism influences not only the ways in which individuals and groups perceive their interests but also how much they can actually gain from cooperation and conflict—and, in this sense, what their "real interests" are. Critics of organizational pluralism who charge it with deforming public consciousness often seem to assume that a "real" common interest exists beneath the deformed state of consciousness and needs only to be perceived in order to be acted on. But this assumption is rarely supported, and

*In the prisoner's dilemma a district attorney puts two suspects in separate rooms, where they cannot communicate, and confronts them with the alternatives of (1) both confessing to the crime and both receiving a lighter sentence; (2) neither confessing and both receiving punishment on a lesser charge, for which a confession is not needed; (3) one getting lenient treatment by confessing and testifying against the other, who receives a maximum sentence.

so far as I know it has never adequately been demonstrated. I want to return briefly to this question in chapter 7.

Our incomplete account of variations in organizational pluralism throws less light, at least directly, on distortions in the public agenda that can reasonably be attributed to organizational pluralism as such. American critics frequently offer as an example the absence of anticapitalist proposals on the public agenda of American political life. It is obvious and undeniable that socialist ideas and political movements do not have a large part in American political controversy and never have. A comparative view, however, shows how mistaken it is to attribute the lack of socialist alternatives to pluralism as such—or, for that matter, to polyarchy as such or to capitalism as such. For in almost every other democratic country, parties advocating socialist ideas, ideals, and solutions have long played a major role in public life—and are, indeed, important elements in the pluralist constellations of these countries. Moreover, since economic enterprises are for the most part privately owned and market oriented in all democratic countries, to attribute the American exception simply to the influence of businessmen is hardly persuasive. At a minimum, a comparative analysis would require one to explain why American businessmen have been so much more influential in preventing the expansion of socialist ideas and organizations than businessmen in Britain, France, Germany, Sweden, Italy, and Japan. To provide an adequate answer to the perplexing and much discussed question of why the United States has been an exception to the general tendency for socialist movements to develop as important participants in the public life of democratic countries would surely require an exploration of the indirect influences of historical experiences and ideology. Whatever the correct explanation may be, however, it is true that, because of the virtual absence of socialist ideas and programs on the American public agenda, Americans are effectively denied the opportunity to consider socialist alternatives in their public discussions. In this sense, one may properly speak, I think, of a distortion of the public agenda in the United States. Although this distortion is not attributable to organizational pluralism as such, it does bear directly on the problem of inequalities in political resources, and I want to return to it in the last chapter.

Different constellations of organizational pluralism do shape public agendas, however, in their consequences for integration and fragmentation. By integration I mean here an arrangement that induces actors in a conflict to consider seriously not only their conflicting interests but also the interests they might have in common; helps them to perceive possibilities for cooperation and to weigh accurately the relative costs and gains of cooperating; reduces the costs of cooperating; and when they perceive cooperation to be advantageous, facilitates their cooperation. Familiar examples of institutions with a weak capacity for integration—or a strongly fragmenting capacity—are the inability of businessmen in a strictly competitive, classically laissez-faire economy to cooperate in order to avoid a depression, and the inability of nations in a strictly competitive international system to avoid a mutually destructive arms race. The morphology of organizational pluralism in some countries supports comparatively strong integrative political and economic institutions. Japan, the Federal Republic of Germany, Norway, and Sweden are recent examples. Conversely, Weimar Germany, the Spanish Republic (1931–1936), Chile (1961–1973), the French Fourth Republic, and Italy furnish examples of relatively extreme fragmentation in political life (Sartori 1976, 131–73; note that Sartori uses the term *polarized pluralism* where I use fragmentation here). The political and economic institutions of the United States are less integrative than those of the first group and less fragmenting than those of the second. As we have just seen, American economic institutions are not highly integrative because they are decentralized and exclusive. American political institutions have never been highly integrative and in some respects they have become more fragmenting in recent years. I shall also come back to this problem in the last chapter.

As to the alienation of final control over the public agenda by citizens and their representatives, our account shows once again that the shape of the problem varies with different constellations of organizational pluralism. Nothing in our account, however, minimizes the importance of the problem. On the contrary, precisely because they make the problem so starkly visible, the systems of corporate pluralism that have evolved in the Scandinavian countries are of particular relevance. There, a significant degree of control over crucial economic decisions, which in conventional democratic theory should remain with the citizens' representatives in parliament and cabinet, has plainly been transferred to a kind of non-elected parliament of industry consisting of the heads of the peak associations. This shift of power away from the elected representatives looks to be irreversible, at least given the institutions of polyarchy—in fact, short of inaugurating an authoritarian regime. I find it hard to resist the conjecture that we are witnessing a transformation in democracy as fundamental and lasting as the change from the institutions of popular government in the city-state to the institutions of polyarchy in the nation-state.

5

More Democracy?

It is sometimes supposed that the problems of pluralism have their origins in the undemocratic nature of many of the governments that exist even in countries governed by polyarchy. The democratization of authoritarian monarchies led to polyarchy; must we not complete the process by democratizing polyarchies? If polyarchies were more fully democratized, one might argue, majorities would govern more effectively; because policies would express majority preferences and interests rather than the mere tugging and hauling among a variety of narrow interest groups, general interests would be better served. Moreover, democratization would go beyond the central government of the state. Other governments would also have to be democratized. Interest organizations would themselves be democratically run, for example; thus all organizations would be more responsive to the general interest of their members rather than, as now, to small oligarchies at the top. To achieve these changes, political resources would have to be distributed much more equitably. A more nearly equal distribution of political resources would require changes in social and economic structures. Democratization presupposes a democratic society.

From this perspective, the defects in democratic pluralism are caused not so much by pluralism or by democracy as by the failure of existing polyarchies to achieve a high level of democracy. In a truly democratic country, the defects of pluralism would tend to disappear.

Because this is an attractive vision, let us take a long leap from reality and try to imagine a country where all the familiar obstacles to voting equality, effective participation, and enlightenment are no longer significant, where the demos is fully inclusive and where it exercises final control over the agenda of decisions. For convenience, let the country have a suitable name: the Democratic Republic. Our imaginary Democratic Republic, then, is an unflawed though large-scale democracy: the government of the state and all other large and relatively autonomous organizations within its boundaries fully satisfy the criteria of the ideal democratic process described in chapter 2. In flat contradiction to universal human experience, I am also going to assume that every adult citizen in the Democratic Republic wholeheartedly believes in the democratic ideal and strives with the utmost dedication to achieve full democratization. There is no discord in Heaven.

Or is there? Even in the Democratic Republic, two questions would have to be answered:

1. In a large-scale democracy, how is political equality among individual citizens to be reconciled with inequalities among organizations?

2. To be sure, the demos exercises final control over the agenda of public affairs—but *what* demos over *what* affairs?

Political Equality: Individuals or Organizations?

The first question arises because of the important role of organizations in large-scale democracy. For example, the criterion of enlightened understanding requires opportunities for discovering and validating one's preferences on matters requiring a collective decision; the criterion of effective participation requires opportunities for expressing one's preferences and the grounds for them. Both kinds of opportunities are more likely to exist in a large system if citizens can participate in organizations. To the extent that access to organizations, and consequently those opportunities, is not equally distributed among citizens, then the criteria of the democratic process are not satisfied. Although the practical solution to this problem is exceptionally difficult, and perhaps impossible, the formal solution is, like many formal solutions in political life, transparently obvious. Let us then assume the following solution to have been carried out satisfactorily:

> *All citizens have and utilize adequate and equal opportunities to participate in organizations.*

Now suppose that, for whatever reasons, some organizations have greater resources than others; that, as a consequence, these organizations have greater influence on decisions; and that, as a further consequence, the preferences of their members count for more than the preferences of citizens who belong to weaker organizations. Then the government of the state does not meet the first criterion of the democratic process—voting equality. It might appear that once again a formal solution would be easy to specify. Suppose we require that:

> *Political resources are effectively regulated (e.g., by limits on expenditures for political purposes) so as to equalize the political resources of all organizations.*

The notion of equalizing the political resources of organizations is, however, ambiguous. If we mean literal *equality among organizations*, an organization with ten members would be entitled to allocate as much to its political efforts as an organization with ten thousand members. if we assume that the same expenditure of political resources results in the same political effectiveness, then each of the ten members of the first organization would have far more influence over decisions than each of the ten thousand members of the second. In general, unless all organizations have an equal number of members, equality among organizations would make it impossible to apply the principle of voting equality to individuals; conversely, if the principle of voting equality is to apply to individuals, it cannot apply to organizations (Dahl and Lindblom 1953, 505). This consequence is inescapable in federal systems, where constituent units— states, provinces, cantons—with unequal population are given equal representation in one chamber of the national legislature; voting equality among states necessarily means voting inequality among citizens. Yet it also exists in systems that are constitutionally unitary but, because of the crucial role played by organizations, in fact combine the "numerical democracy and corporate pluralism" of Norway. Our Democratic Republic, then, faces the following problems: it can satisfy the criterion of voting equality among individual citizens if and only if either (1) no independent organization within the country has any influence on the decisions of the government or (2) the influence of all organizations is proportional to the number of members in each.

Again, the formal solution is easy:

The political resources of all organizations are effectively regulated so that resources are proportional to the number of members.

Yet though this solution is necessary in order to satisfy the criterion of voting equality, in a strict sense it would not be sufficient. For the amount of influence an actor can exert is a function not only of the amount of political resources available but also of skills and incentives. With equal resources available, one actor is likely to gain more influence than another if she uses *more* of her resources, or uses them more *skillfully*, or both. Thus even if the solution were adopted, an organization with more skillful leaders would have more impact on governmental decisions than organizations with politically inept leaders. A satisfactory solution, even if not a formally perfect one, would thus appear to require a very wide diffusion of political skills and probably a serious effort to ensure that every citizen acquired at least minimal political skills. The problem of incentives is far more complex, for the goal of equipping everyone with the same level of incentives (on all questions?) seems highly questionable even as a Utopian ideal.

Even under the artificial assumption that everyone sincerely wants democracy, a formally perfect solution is elusive. However, the solution I have just offered goes so far beyond the experience of any country up to the present time that I may perhaps be excused from pressing further in a sterile quest for a formally perfect but lifeless Utopia.

Final Control: By What Demos?

Democracy offers a paradox: final control over the agenda by one demos necessarily precludes final control over that agenda by any other demos. What is more, final control over a particular matter by one demos necessarily precludes final control over that particular matter by any other demos. To be sure, different democratic organizations can each make decisions about similar agendas, similar matters. What they cannot do is make decisions about precisely the same matter.

The proper *scope* of a democratic organization—the matters it may properly place on its agenda for decision—is dependent on the *domain* of the organization, that is, on the nature of the demos. Matters that are proper for one demos, such as the citizens of a province, are not necessarily proper for another demos, such as the citizens of a village. A large-scale democratic system might meet the criterion of final control in one of two ways: the most inclusive demos could exercise final control and delegate control to various subsystems; or the agenda of each demos could complement others in such a way that, taking into account the agendas of every demos to which each citizen belonged, every citizen is able to partake in final control over the combined agendas. The first solution would be adopted in a state that is, constitutionally speaking, unitary, the second in a constitutionally federal system.

Even among persons fully committed to democracy, however, the proper scope and domain of the democratic process can be a source of conflict, sometimes of highly intense conflict. Let me call these "jurisdictional conflicts." Jurisdictional conflicts are not at all unusual; on the contrary, they are the stuff of everyday political life. They show up, for example, in disputes over the proper scope of national, regional, provincial, state, or local governments. In a country like our Democratic Republic, where economic organizations are democratically controlled, every contested question of economic control, direction, regulation, centralization, decentralization, and so on might produce a jurisdictional dispute. On what grounds could the Democratic Republic arrive at reasonable solutions to its jurisdictional conflicts?

If jurisdictional conflicts truly are the stuff of everyday politics, then whatever constitute good grounds for arriving at reasonable solutions for ordinary political conflicts ought also to constitute good grounds for solving jurisdictional conflicts. The usual grounds for solving ordinary political conflicts are substantive and procedural. Substantive grounds tend to boil down to utilitarian reasons and matters of rights. Given certain rights as fundamental, then within the limits set by these fundamental rights, utilitarian judgments can apply: provided only that fundamental rights be maintained, then let the policy prevail that provides the greatest benefit for the greatest number. Although reasoning from utilitarian considerations in the end conflicts with reasoning from rights, and though neither kind of reasoning invariably produces conclusive answers, these difficulties are not unique to jurisdictional conflicts. In any case, if reasoning does not yield conclusive substantive answers, some process for settling conflicts is required. If this process is held to be proper for making decisions on ordinary matters, then is it not also proper for deciding jurisdictional conflicts? In the Democratic Republic, the process would of course be democratic. And if majority rule were thought to be the proper way to satisfy democratic criteria, then jurisdictional conflicts would also be settled by majority rule.

However, a difficulty lies close beneath the surface: Democratic procedures by which particular demos? A majority of what persons? One solution might be to allow jurisdictional conflicts to be settled by a demos consisting of all citizens whose interests are involved in a significant way. It goes without saying that in practice some set of durable boundaries would have to be established and maintained, and these would often be somewhat arbitrary; yet it

would be excessive to form a new demos to settle every jurisdictional conflict. It is also self-evident that any boundary drawn
around citizens whose interests are involved in a significant way
would have to be at least a little arbitrary. Putting aside these difficulties, however, the solution is not unreasonable. Any demos less
inclusive would deny participation to some qualified citizens whose
interest therefore would probably not be taken equally into account;
and any demos more inclusive would be redundant. If all the citizens in the Democratic Republic believe that the democratic process requires binding decisions to be made according to the principle of majority rule, and if a conflict arises between the majority of a
smaller unit and a majority in a more inclusive unit, such as the Republic itself, then would they not conclude that the majority in the
more inclusive unit ought to have its way? Otherwise, a minority
(even though a majority in a smaller unit) would rule over a majority, which would surely violate the democratic process.

Without further search, then, let us assume that our Democratic Republic adopts the constitutional principle that every jurisdictional conflict is to be settled by democratic procedures among
the largest number of citizens involved. But what if a jurisdictional
conflict involves questions of fundamental rights, rights to independence, self-government, religious freedom? What if majority rule
among citizens in the most inclusive demos leads to the permanent
domination of a majority over a minority? The principle that any
larger group can rightfully dominate any smaller group for no reason
except that it is more numerous is not deducible, so far as I can tell,
from democratic ideas or, for that matter, from any reasonable moral
principles. What makes the majority principle morally acceptable
(when it is acceptable) is one's judgment that the demos consists of
persons who are roughly equal in their qualifications for deciding
the matters on the agenda of the association. But what if a demand
for autonomy by a minority calls that very judgment into question
by asserting a fundamental right or a claim to freedom that the existing demos is not qualified to decide? Suppose we believe that a fun-

damental right or freedom *is* at stake? Something has to give. Is it possible to prescribe a satisfactory *general* solution to fundamental jurisdictional conflicts?

The Problem of a Permanent Majority

As in other countries, in our Democratic Republic the constellation of organizational pluralism will depend in part on a particular pattern of cleavages and conflicts. Consider three possibilities. In Republic A, consensus is so strong and conflicts are so minor that all citizens find the majority principle acceptable for making decisions. On every matter to come before them, an overwhelming majority of citizens agree as to the best alternative. And no citizen is strongly dissatisfied with any outcome or series of outcomes. In Republic B, conflicts are so intense that the majority principle would invariably produce a large dissatisfied minority, although the makeup of the minority would change from decision to decision. In Republic C, polarization is so complete and enduring that the majority principle would produce a permanent minority of highly dissatisfied members. The situation in C, then, looks very much like permanent domination of one group over the other. Yet if Republic C were to operate under strict majority rule, and thus inevitably produce permanent majority dominance, it would seem to meet all the requirements for the democratic process.

However, even if A, B, and C are all fully democratic they are not all equally good for their citizens. For the citizens of Republic A can all achieve their goals more completely than citizens of either B or C. In one meaning of the term, therefore, the citizens of Republic A can be said to enjoy more *freedom* than the citizens of either B or C. If we regard freedom (in this sense) as good, then Republic A, though not more *democratic*, is surely *better* for its citizens than B or C.

Solutions to the problem of minority unfreedom and majority dominance are roughly of two kinds. One is to modify the majority principle. The other is to grant a greater measure of autonomy to the minority. The two solutions are not mutually exclusive. In some countries with deep cultural cleavages both have been used to create consociational rather than majoritarian systems of polyarchy. To be sure, modifying majority rule contradicts the argument that democratic procedures uniquely specify the majority principle, but that argument is doubtful anyway. For example, let us imagine that the citizens of Republic B, agreeing that in their country majority rule would be unfair and would not adequately honor their commitment to democratic principles, choose instead to operate according to a procedure in which the chance of any given outcome is proportional to the number of members supporting it. And in Republic C, in order to avoid the situation of permanent dominance that otherwise would result, the citizens also agree to a lottery, so that about one time out of three the minority view would be likely to prevail. Rules like this may be impractical; but on what grounds can we say that the citizens of B and C do not adhere strictly to democratic procedures?

A Constitutional Principle of Political Autonomy?

The other solution seeks to eliminate domination altogether, and thus to increase freedom, by allowing one or more minorities greater autonomy, perhaps even total independence. Suppose, for example, that in the fragmented situation of Republic B the most intense conflicts result from a religious cleavage. All attempts at complete uniformity of public policy with respect to education, the administration of social security and welfare services, and a number of other matters run afoul of this religious cleavage. After a long search, all the citizens agree to grant the major religious groups a large measure of autonomy on education, social security, and many other matters. Upon removing this major question from collective decision by all the members, conflict is vastly reduced and consensus on the matters now remaining for collective decisions is greatly increased. (This is roughly what happened in the Netherlands with the school pact of 1916–17 and the *verzuiling*, or segmentation, of

Dutch political and social life.) Suppose further that each of the groups now determines its own policies by means of fully democratic procedures. Then the earlier monistic democracy has been transformed into a pluralist democracy.

However, partial autonomy might not be enough. In Republic C the majority and the minority might have so many differences that even with greater autonomy, antagonism and conflict would seriously undermine national consensus. The majority might therefore happily concede independence to the minority. The citizens of each country would now form a more perfect union than before.

It seems hardly open to doubt that in certain circumstances to grant a minority greater autonomy or independence will have favorable consequences for freedom, rights, utilitarian satisfactions, or other values. In both B and C, while a monistic democracy permits a majority of citizens to attain some of their important goals, it prevents a minority from doing so. Autonomy enables the minority of citizens in B to attain their goals within a more decentralized, pluralistic system; complete independence permits the minority in C to do so. In both countries, citizens in the minority are better off after the change. As to the majority of citizens, they would be no worse off if they could still achieve their purposes as well in the new republic as in the old. In fact, because of greater consensus, they might be able to achieve their goals with less conflict, and thus more efficiently, than before. In cases like these, where the old republic was definitely suboptimal in a Paretian sense, the new would be optimal and unequivocally better than the old.

It is tempting to think, therefore, that our Democratic Republic could deal with fundamental jurisdictional controversies by adopting a constitutional principle along these lines: Whenever, as a consequence of democratic procedures, a minority of citizens is persistently deprived by a majority of a fundamental right, freedom, or opportunity, the minority must be granted a degree of autonomy, including independence if need be, sufficient to preserve that right, freedom, or opportunity. To avoid a possible abuse of the principle by citizens less high-minded than we suppose our Democratic Republicans to be, it would help to add a further clause to this effect: Autonomy will be granted only upon a convincing showing that the new unit, whether partly or fully independent, will also meet all the criteria of the democratic process. Let us call these provisions taken together the Constitutional Principle of Political Autonomy. One might object to the ambiguity of key words like *fundamental right, freedom, opportunity*, and so on. We may assume, however, that the Democratic Republic has a constitution in which these are set out firmly enough to permit a supreme court to decide when a minority is entitled to autonomy. Surely the general principle is no more problematical than the constitution under which Americans have governed themselves for nearly two centuries.

Yet a Constitutional Principle of Political Autonomy presents problems. To explore these more deeply, I want to imagine a fundamental jurisdictional conflict over ways of life among organizations that roughly satisfy our Constitutional Principle—something like the demand by French-speaking citizens of Quebec for the independence of the province, let us say. Or let us accept the dreadful anachronism and assume that in 1861 a preponderant majority of Southerners believed that although the time had come to end their peculiar and outworn institution, the society that slavery had helped to create was so distinctive that in order to preserve its best features, even while abandoning slavery, it would be best to separate from the Union. Even if the ex-slaves had been made citizens in the new Confederacy, however, would they not be subject to domination by white majorities on many matters? Blacks were, after all, a minority in the South, and a culturally distinct and disadvantaged minority at that. Is there not every reason to suppose that differences between the white majority and the black minority would have led to the very kind of domination that our Constitutional Principle is intended to prevent? Or take the case of Quebec: would every non-Francophone minority lose its own linguistic rights and privileges and suffer at the hands of the Francophone majority the kind of domination many French-speaking citizens have themselves felt at the hands of the English-speaking majority of Canada?

To anyone prepared to adopt our Constitutional Principle the thought would surely occur that this principle implies another: Political autonomy should be granted only upon a satisfactory showing that the new association will also adopt the Constitutional Principle. What the amendment does, in effect, is to make organizational autonomy a completely overriding value, an absolute right, granted to any minority capable of establishing that (1) its fundamental rights, freedoms, or opportunities are impaired by democratic procedures, and (2) it will itself adhere to democratic procedures in its own government. Is this not finally the answer to the threat of majority tyranny?

It is instructive to consider Lincoln's well-known criticism:

If a minority . . . will secede rather than acquiesce, they make a precedent which in turn will divide and ruin them; for a minority of their own will secede from them whenever a majority refuses to be controlled by such a minority. For instance, why may not any portion of a new confederacy a year or two hence arbitrarily secede again, precisely as a portion of the present Union now claim to secede from it? (Lincoln 1861, 387).

Persuasive as Lincoln's argument is in its appeal to practical judgment, it suffers from a certain theoretical incompleteness. Further secession is unlikely, one might have responded, but if a state should want to leave the proposed Confederacy later on, why should it not be allowed to do so? Lincoln's analysis is not altogether conclusive:

Plainly, the central idea of secession is the essence of anarchy. A majority held in restraint by constitutional checks and limitations, and always changing easily with deliberate changes of popular opinions and sentiments, is the only true sovereign of a free people. Whoever rejects it does, of necessity, fly to anarchy or to despotism. Unanimity is impossible; the rule of a minority, as a permanent arrangement, is wholly inadmissible; so that, rejecting the majority principle, anarchy or despotism in some form is all that is left. (Lincoln 1861, 387).

In one sense, Lincoln was right. Rather than "anarchy," however, he might have said that the central idea of secession—as of our Constitutional Principle—is the essence of the doctrine of *anarchism*. For it would appear to make a state, or any coercive organization, impossible, or at any rate illegitimate, since any group facing coercion on some matter could demand and through secession gain autonomy. Why not accept the solution of "anarchy," or rather anarchism? The answer, it seems to me, is this: *An autonomous organization, even an autonomous and inclusive democracy, may impair the freedom of nonmembers.* Since there is, by definition, no organization outside an autonomous democracy that may properly exercise power to prevent damage to nonmembers, whether or not damage occurs will depend wholly on the actions of the members. As to that, human experience provides little ground for optimism. Thus we are driven to the conclusion that because an increase in organizational autonomy for some persons may adversely affect the rights, freedom, or welfare of others, a reasonable solution to a fundamental jurisdictional conflict would have to provide a way of dealing with significant effects on nonmembers.

It now begins to look as if we have come nearly full circle. If ordinary political conflicts can be settled more or less fairly by the democratic process, I suggested, then ordinary *jurisdictional* conflicts can be. If a procedure like majority rule ordinarily leads to reasonably satisfactory outcomes, while fundamental rights are preserved, then will it not lead to satisfactory outcomes in decisions about jurisdiction? But what if the freedom of a minority is threatened by democratic processes? Granting autonomy to a minority may indeed give it the protection it needs. But while autonomy may in some circumstances protect the rights and welfare of a minority, it may also allow it to do harm to the rights and welfare of others who are not members of the minority—others who may, in fact, constitute a majority of all those whose interests are involved in the conflict. What then is the solution to *this* kind of conflict? Ought we to prescribe that every jurisdictional conflict must be settled by democratic procedures among the largest number of citizens involved? But this was exactly the solution that earlier we found defective.

Is there perhaps a solution to be found in the hallowed democratic principle of *consent*?

Autonomy and Consent
The doctrine of consent was an attempt to draw the fangs of that most coercive of organizations—the state. From the seventeenth century onward, consent was used to provide a moral foundation for the idea of a democratic state. In the democratic theory of the state, only the government of the state had the right to use coercion; but even that government had the right to use coercion only if it was also a democratic government, and then only if it had the consent of its members.

Consent to membership in a state required the fiction of a contract unanimously agreed to by the original members. But the problem of the consent of later generations was singularly vexing. It was often dealt with by the idea of implicit consent. Yet membership in the state was also sometimes portrayed as compulsory, in contrast to voluntary membership in private associations. The fact that membership in a state is compulsory, if it is a fact, provides no rational ground for its being so. Quite the contrary: To say that membership in a state is compulsory simply states the problem. For if membership is really compulsory, then it is not consented to: If it is consented to, it cannot be compulsory.

Let us suppose that in order to preserve the consent of all, the citizens of our Democratic Republic agree to the Constitutional Principle of Unanimous Consent: Every fundamental jurisdictional conflict is to be resolved in a way that has the consent of all the members.

It is hardly surprising that even though he had often used the Principle of Consent to attack slavery, Lincoln does not refer to it anywhere in the First Inaugural. Instead he stands the Principle on its head in order to argue that the original contract of association could not be altered except by unanimous agreement. The astounding conclusion of a mystifying and sometimes inconsistent argument is not that a minority is bound by the original contract, but that nothing less than the consent of *every* state is required to authorize the departure of a *single* state from the Union! Pressed by his obligation, as he thought, to preserve the Union and lacking a well-established rationale anywhere in democratic doctrine, Lincoln was compelled to risk self-contradiction by arguing that coercion may be required in order to insure the consent of all.

By doing so, Lincoln unwittingly revealed a profound difficulty with the Principle. For the Principle leads to prescriptions that are either vacuous or self-contradictory. Prescriptions are vacuous if they apply exclusively to situations in which the members are in fact unanimous; for the problem begins only when conflicts arise. When jurisdictional conflicts exist, if the Principle is interpreted as prescribing that no group of members can ever gain autonomy except with the consent of all, as Lincoln held, the Principle is self-contradictory. For it means that citizenship is compulsory, and being compulsory cannot rest on the consent of those citizens who are compelled, willy-nilly, to remain. Yet if the Principle were interpreted to mean that no democratic organization may ever be denied a claim to autonomy, then a citizen may be forced to "consent" to a grant of autonomy that will harm himself and others. Emptied of all content, the Principle of Consent then becomes vacuous.

Primordial Attachments

In the end, Lincoln's position, like that of Southern secessionists, transcended political reasoning. His ultimate ground was not a rational principle at all, but rather a primordial attachment, to which he appealed in his First Inaugural address when in seeking to dissuade Southerners from the cause of secession he said:

We are not enemies, but friends. We must not be enemies. Though passion may have strained, it must not break our bonds of affection. The mystic chords of memory, stretching from every battlefield, and patriot grave, to every living heart and hearthstone, all over this broad land, will yet swell the chorus of the Union, when again touched, as surely they will be, by the better angels of our nature. (Lincoln 1861, 388)

To Lincoln as to many other Americans the integrity of the Union rested on a transcendant loyalty not reducible to a rational commitment. Beyond some point, loyalties are no longer open to rational discussion. They simply exist; one feels them or not. Is a nonrational loyalty to the integrity of a certain historical collectivity required if democracy is to exist in the government of a state? Probably. It seems doubtful that a country could long exist under a democratic government if its citizen body consisted of merely rational actors acting from conscious and rational "collective" interests.

It seems equally doubtful, however, that a democratic government could long exist in a country where citizens had nothing to hold them together *except* their primordial loyalties. While at some point one's primordial loyalties transcend reason, they need not be wholly inconsistent with conscious and deliberate reason. They are surely more likely to endure when loyalty to one's own people is consistent with loyalty to one's own reasoned principles.

Democratic Dilemmas

We seem to be trapped in a maze where, having reached the end, we discover ourselves at the beginning. Does this not hint at the possibility that large-scale democracy—indeed democracy on any scale—poses some fundamental dilemmas?

First dilemma: rights versus utility. This dilemma runs like a bright thread through all designs for dealing with the problem of democratic pluralism. Are solutions to be judged exclusively on utilitarian grounds, for their contributions to human well-being, welfare, happiness, satisfaction of wants, preferences, volitions, and so on? Are there not also questions of *rights* that are ultimately independent of utilitarian considerations, or at least cannot be finally settled on purely utilitarian grounds? Do not all human beings, for example, possess the fundamental moral *right* to have their interests taken equally into account? Even a utilitarian would acknowledge the validity of the claim to a certain basic moral equality, in insisting that utility to person A counts precisely the same as utility to person B. Thus Bentham's "Each person counts as one and no more than one" (Mill 1962, p. 319).

But beyond this fundamental right there are others that might conflict with a utilitarian judgment. Does a people have a fundamental right to govern itself? If so, does not this fundamental right require all the subsidiary rights implied by the right of self-government? Are rights like these justified on other grounds? Must not utilitarian considerations therefore sometimes yield to considerations of rights?

Tested by mental experiments in the realm of hypothetical cases, it appears impossible to discover any right that can reasonably be justified in utter disregard for its consequences for the well-being of persons affected by the exercise of that right—including the possessor. Yet it is equally unreasonable to contend that rights must *always* give way to utilitarian considerations. Can we justify executing innocent prisoners in order to set an example to others? Is this not a violation of a human right so fundamental that it cannot be justified on utilitarian grounds?

Moral philosophers have struggled endlessly with this dilemma. (For one solution, see Scanlon 1978.) Utilitarians remain convinced that they have successfully disposed of their critics' arguments. But they have failed to convince a substantial body of other philosophers. What is true of moral philosophy is a fortiori true of political life, as we are now about to see.

Second dilemma: a more exclusive versus a more inclusive demos. In practice, every demos is exclusive; no demos, no matter how large, has ever included all human beings. There simply is not and never has been an association of all human beings governed by the democratic process—or, for that matter, any single government.

The question arises: Why this demos rather than another? Might it not properly be more inclusive—or more exclusive? The question seems to admit of no definitive answer. That answers can be reached at all is the half-concealed mystery of democratic ideas and practices. The question is, in fact, an embarrassment to all normative theories of democracy, or would be were it not ignored. In practice, solutions call not upon theoretical reason, which is baffled by the question, but, as with Lincoln, on primordial attachments to tribe, town, city, subculture, nation, country. Though it is sometimes held that a more inclusive demos is always preferable to a less inclusive one, the argument is patently defective. For the argument logically implies that the only proper demos is all of humanity. But even those who defend an inclusive demos invariably accept, and without serious questioning, the limits on the demos imposed by primordial or historical boundaries—which nowadays are those of nation or country. But why draw the boundaries of the demos at the borders of a country? On the other hand, why not? Suppose we agree that maximum inclusion today really means the largest demos within the historically (and often arbitrarily) given boundaries of a country. There is still the second embarrassment: No demos has ever included children, and those who contend that a more inclusive demos is better than a less inclusive one have no intention of demanding that children be included.

That no one seriously insists that the demos be *completely* inclusive suggests hidden premises at work. One kind of hidden premise often turns out to be utilitarian or expediential: demos X is better than Y because it leads to greater well-being, utility, satisfaction of preferences, welfare, happiness. An assumption of this kind is heir to all the usual defects of utilitarian moral reasoning. However elegant the efforts to quantify the relative utilities, or whatnot, the comparison never in practice leads to anything like an uncontestable conclusion. The quantities, even if precise, are fictitious; in fact, the greater their precision, the greater the fiction. There are also the usual problems of intensity and quality: *is* pushpin as good as poetry, *is* the satisfied fool better than Socrates dissatisfied? And there is the eternal challenge of nonutilitarian moral standards: rights, duties, personal integrity.

Both utilitarian and nonutilitarian arguments can be readily used either way: to justify a more inclusive demos or a more exclusive one. In the end, no solution to the problem can be better than the solution to the conflict between utilitarian and nonutilitarian moral standards.

Third dilemma: equality among individuals versus equality among organizations. The principle of equality in voting, which is central to the idea of democracy, refers to human beings, persons, individuals. Except under certain rare and all but irrelevant circumstances, the principle of voting equality is necessarily violated whenever units, associations, organizations, states, provinces, or countries, rather than individual persons, are granted equal votes. For, as we saw, unless the number of citizens is identical in all the units, then voting equality among units means inequality of votes among citizens. Except in rare cases, the number of citizens is not the same in all the units; if it were, there would be no reason to reject the principle of voting equality for the principle of organizational equality.

Should the principle of voting equality among citizens never be modified in order to allow for greater political equality among organizations (and so less among citizens)? Should a national legislature be designed to represent only citizens, or only provinces or states, or both? The American constitutional solution was, of course, to do both. Ought there to be functional representation? If so, should votes in a functional body be allocated according to the number of citizens in each functional group, in which case the body would not be all that different from one based on territorial constituencies; or should they be allocated equally among certain types of organizations, thereby violating the criterion of voting equality among citizens? Proponents of functional representations have never met this dilemma satisfactorily. Either their solution violates the principle of voting equality on grounds they are unable to justify; or else it does not, and if not, then functional representation offers few advantages over territorial representation.

The question remains: Is it ever justified to permit equality among organizations at the expense of equality among individual citizens? Arguments for doing so rest on considerations both of utility—indeed, often of expediency—and of rights. Systems of democratic corporatism, like the corporate pluralism of the Scandinavian countries, are thought to be justified because they are useful. Is there a better way to arrive at decisions involving the great nationwide interest organizations? Unless the government acts with the consent of the organizations, it is impotent. It cannot *impose* a solution. As is well known, cabinet officers and troops cannot mine coal. But if parliament *is* to act with the consent of the interest organizations, then some system of corporate pluralism seems necessary. But corporate pluralism means, to quote Rokkan once again, that votes count but organizational resources decide. Likewise, consociational democracies may permit any one of several groups to veto policies its leaders think harmful. In effect, consociational democracy requires unanimity among certain major social aggregates and their organizations. These arrangements are held to be justified, not only because of their utility in gaining widespread consent in a segmented society, but also because they guarantee the *right* of each group to have its fundamental interests taken into account. Do Catholics and Calvinists, socialists and liberals, all have an equal right to their own subculture and community life? Do Francophone Walloons and Dutch-speaking Flemish have an equal right to their language and traditions? Should members of the small Italian-speaking minority in Switzerland have the same rights to cultural autonomy as members of the larger French- and German-speaking minorities? In the United Nations General Assembly, all countries are given equal votes. Is this justified only out of expediency, or is it also a matter of right? Would any foreseeable world government, even one much more nearly ideal than the U.N., operate exclusively under a system of majority rule where the demos consists simply of the human species? I do not say that satisfactory answers can never be found. But clearly there is a conflict of fundamental principles.

Fourth dilemma: uniformity versus diversity. As these examples suggest, diversity is precious, not only to groups that prize their own ways, religion, language, place, customs, traditions, history, and values, but also to everyone who holds that human diversity is good in itself or in its results. The protection of diversities can be justified on utilitarian grounds: It yields more satisfaction (or whatever) than uniformity—especially when one adds the costs of suppressing differences valued by their possessors. Protecting diversity can also be justified because one has a right to one's own identity, personhood, personality, culture. Am I to be punished because I insist on speaking my mother tongue? Do I not have a *right* to be different in that way from the majority of my fellow citizens?

In the modern world it is an easy and congenial task to defend diversity. If the idea of uniformity is superficially less attractive, uniformity is nonetheless desirable because not all differences among human beings are matters of right or have good consequences. Do we not advocate uniformity in the protection of fundamental rights? Oppose differences in the right of citizens to vote, to have a fair trial? When differences infringe on basic rights, one's appreciation of diversity crumbles. Should neighborhoods that want to preserve their special character be allowed to exclude anyone who does not fit in? There is also the question of the level at which differences ought to be permitted or protected: at the level of the individuals or the level of the group? If at the group level, what kind of group? With respect to what kinds of differences? To be sure, sometimes protection at the individual level necessarily requires protection at the group level. Religion is ordinarily not only a personal activity: It is social and organizational as well. Consequently, a government cannot protect the right of individuals to their religious beliefs without protecting their right to adhere to diverse religious organizations, to practice their rites in the presence of their coreligionists, and to exclude from membership those who reject the sect's beliefs. Applied to racial differences the same reasoning would require us to tolerate racial segregation in a neighborhood, school, university, workplace, trade union.

Equality means, precisely, identity. If A and B are to be treated as equal with respect to a thing of value, a right, opportunity, duty, or share in some social allocation, then the thing must be identical for A and B. If A and B have an equal right to vote, A's right to vote is identical with B's: the rights of A and B are theoretically inter-changeable. Obviously, equality conflicts with diversity. In the steady march of the idea of equality throughout history that Tocque-ville believed he discerned at work as a fundamental force in the world, many kinds of differences once widely thought acceptable are no longer. What might from an earlier perspective be justified as a proper difference, a desirable or ineradicable diversity, becomes an unjustified inequality, discrimination, unfairness, inequity. If equality is often desirable, then so is uniformity.*

Fifth dilemma: centralization versus decentralization. Uniformity and diversity: centralization and decentralization. Although the two sets of terms are not symmetrical, uniformity often requires some centralization, and diversity often presupposes some de-centralization. Let me now specify more precisely what I mean by centralization and decentralization. Suppose that subsystems exist within a more inclusive system of controls. Then the inclusive system—for the moment let me refer to it simply as the organization—is decentralized to the extent that the subsystems are autonomous in relation to other subsystems in the organization. If one subsys-tem controls all the others with respect to x, then with respect to x it is a center and the organization is centralized with respect to x. Sometimes one subsystem controls all the others over a large range of crucial actions. A subsystem of this kind might be designated *the* Center of the organization. Starting from any given situation, then, to decentralize means to increase the autonomy of subsystems in re-lation to *the* Center or *a* center. By definition, decentralization also

---

*The argument of this paragraph is presented in terms of what Rae et al. call "lot-regarding equality." However, uniform enforcement would also be required for "person-regarding equality," where (as in the case of handicapped persons) a concern for equal treatment of the different needs of different persons would require their receiving unequal "lots." Though the two kinds of equality are in fundamental con-flict, each would justify uniformity in application. Cf. Rae et al. (1981).

means a decrease in control over the subsystems by a center, and in particular *the* Center. To centralize means exactly the reverse: when a center's control over subsystems increases, subsystem autonomy decreases. Since an organization may be centralized with respect to some matters and decentralized with respect to others, it is obvious that patterns of organization can be extraordinarily complex—a fact painfully familiar to all experienced students of organizations.

For example, every subsystem in the organization might be highly controlled by *a* center; in this sense the organization is highly centralized and might well appear so from the viewpoint of a member of any of the subsystems. But each of the centers might be relatively autonomous in relation to the others: in this sense, each center is also a somewhat independent subsystem. Thus the organization, though centralized, would be collegial rather than monocratic. To describe it in a different way: Control would be centralized in the joint leadership of the centers, but not among the leaders.

If organizations were the mechanisms of pure rationality they were often pictured to be in early theories of organization, and if centralization and decentralization had no other significant consequences than those immediately entailed in shifting control over certain matters toward or away from the Center, then a choice between centralization or decentralization would doubtless be simpler than it usually is. However, organizations are rarely if ever mechanisms of pure rationality; they are not constituted merely of rational actors striving only to maximize the efficient attainment of the organization's official goals. In practice, organizations depart from a model of pure rationality in several ways. For one thing, centralization and decentralization have consequences for communication, and thus for control. Centralized control requires a flow of accurate communications toward the Center. Centralized communication systems are not only in danger of jamming up from overload; they are highly susceptible to distortion. After the king executes the first messenger who brings bad tidings, the word quickly gets around.

By decentralizing decisions to autonomous units, lengthy lines of communication can be shortened and the jam-up at the center can be reduced. But the big picture, the synoptic overview, may be destroyed; each unit makes its decisions without much awareness of what is happening elsewhere.

Centralization and decentralization also have consequences for power beyond those described in models of pure rationality. To centralize control is not merely to allocate resources for influencing others to a perfectly neutral incumbent of some central office. Centralization puts resources in the hands of specific human beings at the Center, persons with goals of their own. To decentralize is to allocate resources of influence away from the Center, and thus to convey them to other specific human beings. The problem is, of course, that these actors may very well not devote their resources simply to the ostensible purpose of the exercise, to see that the prescribed goals of the organization are attained more efficiently. They may also use their resources for their own particular purposes. They usually do. It is not going too far to say that leaders almost always use some of the resources available to them for self-aggrandizement. This is the essence of Acton's famous aphorism that power tends to corrupt, and absolute power corrupts absolutely. Is it reasonable to expect that any human beings, any team, group, sect, party, or stratum will long refrain from using the resources available to them in order to enhance their own distinct interests? Even where democratic forms remain, to allocate large resources to the Center may lead to a loss of control by citizens. Conversely, to shift resources away from the Center to more autonomous subsystems may prevent domination by the Center, but as we saw in chapter 3, decentralization may also allow domination *within* each subsystem.

In political life, at least, to centralize or decentralize is never simply a problem in engineering, where the strengths and tolerances can be nicely determined. It is a problem in political dynamics, where the consequences can only be guessed at. To increase the authority of the Presidency always increases the power of a person, or a group of people, in the White House. Decentralization to local communities increases the power of certain people more or less resident in certain localities. Although it is always uncertain how these various persons will use their power, human experience supports the hunch that they will use some of it to advance their own interests. And these interests may prove to be sharply adverse to the interests of others.

Sixth dilemma: concentration versus dispersion of power and political resources. Uniformity, centralization, concentration of power and resources; diversity, decentralization, dispersion of power and resources. If the last triad is the program of classical liberalism, what is the first? Liberalism, and in particular liberal ideas about democracy, were formulated in opposition to concentrated power. Liberal democracy represented a movement away from the uniformity of centralized regulation imposed by means of power concentrated in the crown, the royal ministers, and an unrepresentative parliament. By Tocqueville's time the liberal strategy had been so successful in the United States that it was necessary to sound a new liberal warning: By concentrating all power in the people, or rather in majorities, democracy also posed grave risks to liberty, most of all in a country where the citizens were more nearly equal in their conditions than had ever been true before among any numerous body of people.

The hostility of liberalism to concentration of power runs deep; as has often been observed, it may run deepest in that country where liberal ideas have always confronted the weakest challenge. Yet even in the United States, liberalism in the twentieth century yielded up a great deal of its earlier commitment to dispersion. Progressive liberalism, reform liberalism, the liberalism of Woodrow Wilson's New Freedom and Franklin Roosevelt's New Deal, all demanded that certain national policies be enforced uniformly throughout the United States. As a direct consequence, the new liberalism sought greater centralization of control over policies and decisions in federal agencies and a greater concentration of political resources at centers in Washington. Even more important, reform liberals quickly discovered that without strong presidential leadership no reform program could fight its way past the elaborate combination of check-points built into the American political process. These, of course, gave great advantages to defenders of the status quo. Liberal reform therefore required that political resources be concentrated in the hands of the president. Richard Nixon did not create the Imperial Presidency; he inherited it. In point of fact it was mainly liberals, not their conservative opponents, who designed, encouraged, supported, and brought about the shift of resources to the White House that finally facilitated the creation of an Imperial Presidency.

If this change took place in a country where hostility to concentrated power was stronger than elsewhere, the same process was bound to occur in other countries where the political traditions were far less monolithically liberal. It is a commonplace, but a valid one, to say that in all democratic countries concentration of power in the executive branch and the central bureaucracies has vastly increased in this century. Although the institutions of polyarchy have not collapsed under this new weight, it would be wrong to say that anxieties about the consequences of concentration have thereby been shown to be irrational. For one thing, the flourishing of dictatorships, sometimes in the extreme form of totalitarian rule, has once again demonstrated that democracy depends on a dispersion of power and resources.

Is this antinomy—concentration versus dispersion of power and resources—rather more lopsided than the others? Are we all really in favor of dispersion? Not necessarily. Once we accept the premise that there must be definite even if not perfectly clear limits to concentration in a polyarchy, then within these limits the dilemma becomes perfectly real.

For whenever (a) uniform enforcement of a policy is desirable, (b) uniformity cannot be attained without centralization, and (c) centralization requires a concentration of power and resources, then either one must forego a desirable uniformity or else accept concentration. Everyone who is not an anarchist is likely to agree that the risks of concentration are sometimes offset by the advantages of a uniform policy. The conflict between the advantages and risks of concentration is genuine, and citizens and leaders cannot escape the force of this dilemma in any democratic country.

Even in our imaginary Democratic Republic the people's chorus will not sing eternally in perfect harmony. Like all existence, political life in a democracy can pose hard choices to its citizens. But hard choices are still choices. The dilemmas and difficulties described in this chapter do not justify inaction. They are simply considerations to be taken into account in clarifying the alternatives before us. Human problems have better and worse solutions. Because of the difficulties described in this chapter, even the better solutions will usually have disadvantages, sometimes grave ones. But to say that a solution has disadvantages is never a good reason for preferring the worse to the better.

In order to clarify the limits on solutions to the problem of democratic pluralism set by democracy itself, I began this chapter by imagining a Democratic Republic that meets democratic criteria perfectly. But we all know that the institutions, processes, and conditions of polyarchy in democratic countries fall far short of meeting democratic criteria. Among other things, we know that in the real world political resources of many kinds—knowledge, information, skill, access to organizations, income, wealth, and status, among others—are unequally distributed among citizens. We know also that patterns of inequality in resources like .these are not the same in all democratic countries.

Historically, democratization has meant redistributing political resources, reducing political inequalities. While further democratization can never be free of disadvantages, as long as great inequalities in political resources persist democratic pluralism must fail to attain the potentialities of large-scale democracy.

6

Redistributing Wealth and Income: Capitalism and Socialism

Democracy is and has always been closely associated in practice with private ownership of the means of production. It is an arresting fact that even today in *every* country governed by polyarchy the means of production are for the most part owned "privately." * Conversely, *no* country where the means of production are owned mainly by the state or (as under the Yugoslav constitution) by "society" is governed by polyarchy. To put it schematically, there are no examples in reality of (d) in table 3. If by capitalism we mean an economic order in which the instruments of production are mainly owned privately, then to what extent are organizational pluralism and its problems simply consequences of capitalism?

Capitalism, Socialism, and Pluralism

It seems hardly open to question that industrial capitalism stimulates the growth of organizations. What is more, the prevailing belief system of capitalism in the nineteenth century purported to show that for economic units, very nearly complete autonomy from external controls by government or other economic organizations was necessary and desirable in order to achieve a just and progressive society. To classical economists, a rational economic order required that enterprises be subject internally to the exclusive control of the owner or entrepreneur, who in turn must be almost entirely

---

*They are also all "market-oriented." Cf. Lindblom (1977, 161).

TABLE 3. Polyarchy and Social Ownership

		Country is governed by polyarchy:	
		Yes	No
Means of production are mainly owned:	Privately	(a)	(b)
	Socially	(d)	(c)

free of direct control by actors outside the firm, including the government, and at the same time subject to the overwhelming influence of the market. In the theory of economic liberalism, all strictly unilateral controls vanished, sweeping dominance cleanly out of every economic relationship. Control, authority, power were concepts of no theoretical significance in neoclassical theory. In the final analysis, all economic relationships dissolved into contracts freely and rationally consented to by autonomous individuals. In the theoretical imagination, then, the difference between anarchism and economic liberalism was at times paper thin—so thin that a special form of anarchism was to arise that simply carried economic individualism one critical step further and got rid of the state entirely.

As untold generations of neophyte economists have learned, the pure theory of competition, which furnished the main theoretical grounds for the desirability of unregulated capitalism, sought to demonstrate how the almost total autonomy of the firm and the near absence of all external controls were justified, provided only that each individual enterprise was small relative to the total market, hence unable to influence prices, hence completely responsive to the cues of the market, and so (as the pure theory came to be elaborated with marvelous intellectual elegance and refinement) exquisitely subject to the ultimate sovereignty of the consumer. The obligation of the state, then, was to ensure competition by preventing combinations, monopolies, and other interferences with the market. Except for the state's guarantee of the framework itself, the system was practically self-regulating.

How closely practice approached theory even during the high tide of laissez-faire is a matter of controversy. Among different countries, certainly, there were important variations in the extent to which governments continued to regulate economic units; and in every country where capitalism flourished, advocates of stronger controls and even the displacement of capitalism by some alternative economic order made their views heard and often influenced government policies.

In no country did the self-regulating market economy completely prevail, or if it did, not for long. Everywhere the evolution of capitalism witnessed a reduction in the autonomy of economic organizations and a corresponding increase in controls exercised by both governments and other economic units. Whatever may have been the reality in the nineteenth century, the twentieth saw the emergence of giant corporations whose governments in both their internal and their external relations took on many of the characteristics of the governments of states. The giant corporation thus became, de facto, if not yet de jure, both a *public* enterprise and a *political* system. Because giant corporations bear only an illusory resemblance to the relatively small, competitive firms completely subject to the market in classical and neoclassical theory, private ownership and the autonomy of the enterprise can no longer draw much reasoned support from the hypothetical virtues sustained by an increasingly less relevant model. On the contrary, alternative models of a progressive, just, rational, or otherwise desirable economic order deserve consideration. Among these alternative possibilities, obviously some will include systems with much stronger hierarchical controls exercised by the government of the state.

It is reasonable to ask, then, whether a high degree of organizational pluralism is, at least in modern times, so exclusively a product of capitalism that it would necessarily disappear in an economic order that treated giant firms both in theory and practice as *public* enterprises and *political* systems. In particular, would organizational pluralism decline significantly in an order where the principal means of production were socially rather than privately owned, that is, in a socialist economic order?

Although such a view is widely held, it seems to me mistaken, because it rests upon a theoretical confusion that makes *ownership* equivalent to *control*. Advocates of capitalism, like their socialist critics, have often assumed that private ownership is both a necessary and a sufficient condition for control of the enterprise by the owners; conversely, ownership by the government of the state is thought to be both a necessary and a sufficient condition for control by the government of the state. It is assumed that if an enterprise is privately owned, then of course the owners make the key decisions, either directly or through managers who are no more than agents. If enterprises are owned by society, or the government, or the people, or the workers, then it must follow that the decisions of the enterprises will be made by society, the government, the people, the workers.

Experience in this century, however, has demonstrated that ownership is definitely not a *sufficient* condition for control. One cannot even be certain how much a particular form of control requires a particular form of ownership. Systems based on state or social ownership range all the way from the highly hierarchical system of managerial dominance in the Soviet Union, where even trade unions are of negligible importance, to self-management of enterprises as it has been practiced in Yugoslavia. Between these extremes the combinations of internal and external controls in the publicly owned enterprises of other countries are of almost infinite variation. Recent experience also exhibits wide variation in the control systems of privately owned enterprise, though whether full-scale self-management by all who work for an enterprise is possible with private ownership remains to be demonstrated in practice. In addition, of course, there are an enormous number of possible (and existing) combinations of private and public ownership, and mixtures of governmental, market, consumer, and enterprise controls over decisions.

If we accept the axiom that in general a specific form of ownership is not a sufficient condition for a specific control relationship (and may not be a necessary condition), then the question of control is theoretically prior to the question of ownership. Seen in this perspective, what capitalism did in theory, and in substantial measure in practice, was to inaugurate a system of decentralized control over economic organizations that were to a high degree autonomous vis-à-vis the central government and one another. If socialism by definition entails social ownership of economic enterprises, and unless by definition it must be centralized, then a socialist economy could be highly decentralized and therefore organizationally pluralistic. A socialist government might grant extensive autonomy to enterprises in order to permit internal controls much more democratic than exist either under capitalism or in centralized socialist systems like the USSR. Obviously no socialist government—probably no government—would eliminate all external controls, whether by markets, the government of the state, or both. A decentralized socialist order might nonetheless generate just as much organizational pluralism as exists in any nonsocialist order, and perhaps a good deal more.

Nor is organizational pluralism in a socialist order necessarily at odds with Marxism. On this as on so many other questions the corpus of Marx's work is, as a whole, ambiguous. For half a century, Marxists who looked to the Soviet Union as the very embodiment of Marxist verities assumed that a socialist order must necessarily operate as a centralized command economy. Yet some passages in Marx—particularly his well-known description of the Paris Commune, which he praised as "the political form at last discovered under which to work out the economical emancipation of labor"—lend eloquent support to the idea that socialism would be highly decentralized (Marx 1974a, 210–12).

To put the matter schematically again, both in its classical form and to a considerable extent even in its highly developed form, capitalism is represented by (a') in table 4. While the influence of Soviet theory and practice has tended to identify socialism with (c'), in principle socialism might also be represented by (d'). But is (d')

TABLE 4. Centralization and Ownership

		In relation to any single national center firms are:	
		Moderately or highly autonomous (decentralized)	Highly controlled (centralized)
Means of production are mainly owned:	Privately	(a')	(b')
	Socially	(d')	(c')

only a theoretical category? It definitely exists in at least one case: Yugoslavia. And unless one is prepared to argue that by definition the Yugoslav economy is privately owned and that by definition Yugoslav Marxists are not genuine Marxists, one is compelled to agree that socialism and Marxism as interpreted by some Marxists are compatible with a high degree of organizational pluralism (Cf. Rusinow 1977).

To understand the crucial alternatives for both the political and the economic order, then, one must focus first on control and second on ownership. In sorting out economic alternatives, the key question is not whether an order is socialist or nonsocialist, whether enterprises are owned "privately" or "publicly" (though these may be important secondary questions), but how much autonomy is permitted to economic enterprises and the nature of internal and external controls. A nonsocialist, privately owned economy can be dominated by an authoritarian political order that closely regulates the activities of economic enterprises, as in Nazi Germany during wartime. Conversely the experience of Yugoslavia, even if it is unique up to now, demonstrates that a socialist economic order can be highly decentralized and pluralistic.

A shift from "private" to "social" ownership then, need not *necessarily* reduce the amount of organizational pluralism in a country. It is altogether possible that in some countries (the United States might be one) where important decisions are strongly influenced by giant corporations hierarchically dominated by their managers, the inauguration of a decentralized socialist economy—in which, for example, economic enterprises were democratically governed by a demos consisting of all persons employed by the firm—would result in an increase, not a decrease, in the number and autonomy of economic organizations.

The upshot of this discussion is this: The amount of organizational pluralism in a country does not appear to depend on whether enterprises are privately or socially owned. It does depend on the extent to which decisions are decentralized, that is, on the amount of autonomy permitted to enterprises. And the amount of autonomy permitted to enterprises appears to be theoretically independent of forms of ownership, hence of capitalism and socialism as such. A capitalist order may be, but need not be, highly decentralized. A socialist order may be, but need not be, highly centralized (Cf. Dahl 1971, 57ff.).

Because capitalism has prevailed in all democratic countries up to now, it is hard to untangle the effects on organizational pluralism of the major structural variables: the economic structures of capitalism, on the one hand, and the political structures of polyarchy, on the other. That each makes an independent contribution is supported by a simple mental experiment employing the categories of table 5. Although all democratic countries have capitalist economic orders (a.1), not all countries with capitalist economic orders are "democratic," i.e., governed by polyarchal institutions (c.1). However, the democratic countries have many more relatively independent *political* organizations than the nondemocratic countries. Our mental experiment thus confirms the argument of chapter 3 that the institutions of polyarchy stimulate organizational pluralism, quite aside from the economic order. As to the effects of the economic order, in this chapter I have argued that economic decentralization to relatively autonomous enterprises also makes an independent contribution to organizational pluralism. Although (a.2) is empty because in no democratic country are most means of production socially owned, a few socialist countries with relatively decentralized

TABLE 5. Polyarchy, Decentralization, and Ownership

Control over enter-prises and firms is:	Country is governed by polyarchy:	
	Yes	*No*
Moderately or extremely decentralized		
Privately owned	a.1. All Polyarchies	c.1. Many authoritarian countries: Argentina, Chile, Brazil, South Africa, etc.
Socially owned	a.2. No cases	c.2. Yugoslavia (Hungary?)
Highly centralized		
Privately owned	b.1. War-time economies: Britain, U.S.	d.1. War-time economies: Nazi Germany, Italy, Austria, Japan
Socially owned	b.2. No cases.	d.2. USSR, other Ea. European countries

economics, such as Yugoslavia and perhaps Hungary, provide a test by analogy.

How important is the contribution to pluralism made by the institutions and practice of polyarchy in comparison with that of economic decentralization? Something of a test case is provided by the wartime experiences of Britain and the United States, when for several years the economies were tightly run by centralized direction, while the main institutions of polyarchy remained mostly intact. In the short run at least, a large number of crucial organizations—political, cultural, religious—retained a significant degree of autonomy even though social as well as economic institutions were to some extent mobilized for war. It is difficult to say what the effects on organizational autonomy and polyarchy itself would be if peacetime economic decisions were for several generations as highly centralized as in the wartime economies of Britain and the United States. Since centralized direction of the economy is sometimes recommended, and might in some circumstances seem to have great advantages over decentralization, I now want to turn to the question of centralization.

Redistribution by Selective Centralization

An economic order in keeping with the decentralist thrust of polyarchy would be an economy in which a great many decisions were decentralized to subsystems and only a few crucial, strategic decisions were made centrally. Such an order might have several variants, both capitalist and socialist. In one important variant, the economic order would be essentially what it already is in democratic countries. Most enterprises would be privately owned, market-oriented, and more or less competitive. But certain kinds of crucially important decisions would be made centrally. Among these would be certain decisions bearing on inequalities.

However, is this not exactly what happened in most democratic countries in the decades following the Great Depression? Is this not simply a prescription for "government intervention," a welfare state, a mixed economy, selective controls, fine tuning of the economy, and the other familiar policies and techniques of governments in countries governed by polyarchy? It is arguable, however, that in all democratic countries government intervention has developed rather haphazardly. Government policies are an accretion of many decades of incremental changes, particular conflicts, obsolete political coalitions, inconsistent and outdated ideas and programs, and so on. The result is both unselective and excessive centralization and unselective and insufficient decentralization.

In this view, the task is to identify a very small range of strategic policies and make sure that they are enacted and carried out. When these strategic policies are functioning properly, much of the central apparatus of existing welfare states can be dismantled. To be sure, decentralization to more autonomous subsystems—individuals, families, state and local governments, associations, firms, and so on—will inevitably have its costs. But these costs will be far outweighed by the advantages of decentralization—provided only that certain strategically important decisions are made centrally.

What strategic matters require centralized decision? It is perfectly obvious that one of the most influential structures in any society is the distribution of income and wealth. Disparities of income and wealth confer extraordinary advantages and disadvantages. The distribution of advantages and disadvantages is often arbitrary, capricious, unmerited, and unjust, and in virtually all advanced countries no longer tolerable. Because the consequences are no longer tolerable, governments have been compelled to adopt policies intended to alter either the distribution of income and wealth or its consequences, or both.

In a privately owned, market-oriented economy, however, the decisions that mainly determine the distribution of wealth and income are for the most part decentralized. To reduce and regulate the effects of unequal incomes and wealth without doing much to control the cause itself contributes to the extensive regulatory apparatus of the welfare state and the infinite varieties of government intervention, subsidy, and compensation intended to offset the disadvantages suffered by the worst off and the advantages gained by the best off. Why not go directly to the heart of the problem by enforcing centralized policies that would ensure a more equitable distribution of wealth and income? Straightforward taxation of incomes, inheritance, and wealth would accomplish with a small bureaucracy and low public outlays for regulation what cannot be accomplished successfully by the vast centralized bureaucracies characteristic of contemporary governments.

We might then sum up the solution of redistribution by selective centralization along these lines: Unjustifiable differences in incomes and wealth would be eliminated by central government taxation and transfer payments. However, the ways in which individual citizens and families could spend their economic resources would go largely unregulated by the central government. Although freedom in personal expenditure would have some adverse consequences, the disadvantages would be more than outweighed by the relative advantages of diversity, decentralization, and dispersion over uniformity, centralization, and concentration.

There is much to be said for this solution. Many of the policies in modern welfare states have treated the symptoms of maldistribution but not the maldistribution itself. This is most clearly so in the United States, where the distribution of wealth and income has never steadily been a salient political issue; and neither major party has ever consistently pressed for substantial redistribution. American civic orientations and the absence of a substantial socialist movement reinforce one another and help to maintain the low salience of the issue. (I return to this point in the last chapter.) By contrast, in other countries labor and socialist parties have sometimes made economic redistribution a major issue; in some, taxation and transfer payments have brought about substantial changes in the distribution of income and wealth.

Like every other proposal, no doubt, redistribution by selective centralization raises a number of questions, of which several are particularly germane here. Precisely because the solution selects one strategic policy for centralized control, is it thereby much *too* selective? Are there not many matters of equal importance that would still not be adequately dealt with? Would these matters not also require some measure of centralized control? One immediately thinks of foreign affairs, international control of nuclear weapons, foreign trade, military policy and procurement, nuclear energy, economic stability and growth, undesirable externalities of economic enterprises, political and civil rights, environmental problems . . . And would a centralized social security system no longer be desirable? If these and other matters require centralized control, then the principle of *selective* centralization may have to be abandoned. Certainly in countries where governments have been the most vigorous in redistribution by means of taxation and transfer payments, central governmental controls have also increased over a very broad range of matters. Some of this expansion no doubt reflects a lack of commitment to selective as against general centralization, and an earlier if now declining optimism about centralization, particularly on the part of labor and socialist parties. But does it not also reflect the fact that many strategic decisions need to be centralized?

In addition, the solution of selective centralization sharply poses the question of limits on redistribution set by the institutions and orientations of a market-oriented, privately owned economy, that is, of capitalism. The problem I have in mind is not so much the well-worn issue of incentives but rather political resistance to extensive redistribution. In redirecting flows of income by means of income taxes and transfer payments, a government is in the position of taking income already allocated to one set of recipients by the economic institutions and politically reallocating it to different sets of recipients. To the extent that civic orientations are "bourgeois" or "capitalist" and the economic institutions are thought to be generally desirable, the initial recipients tend to see redistribution as unjustly taking their wealth or income away and giving it to others, in short, as political robbery. So long as redistribution can be achieved by steep income taxes on a very small minority then the majority principle readily lends itself to redistribution. But as the minority grows in size, the chances also increase that a majority coalition will be formed against further redistribution. Why should the great bulk of the voters in the middle ranges of the income distribution coalesce with the poor in *favor* of further distribution rather than with the rich *against* further distribution? If civic orientations stimulate the pursuit of rational egoism rather than altruism or generalized benevolence, then a rationally self-interested majority coalition is likely to oppose further redistribution well before equality of incomes is approached. The Scandinavian countries have probably already reached this point.

The United States, however, is a long way from having achieved the redistributive policies of the Scandinavian countries. Here the constitutional and political institutions operate, in no small measure by design, to weaken majority rule and heighten the effectiveness of minorities in resisting changes, particularly, of course, minorities well endowed with political resources. In addition, civic orientations about property rights and private ownership, which formed when the country was predominantly a nation of farmers, strengthen the view of redistribution as an illicit appropriation of income from some in order to bring about an unjustifiable transfer to others.

Thus in both the Scandinavian countries and the United States, political limits on redistribution are set by civic orientations. Can these orientations be changed sufficiently to achieve redistribution within a privately owned, market-oriented economy? Or would the solution of redistribution by selective centralization be fully realizable only in a country with socialist institutions and a widespread "socialist consciousness"?

Redistribution by a Centrally Directed Economy

Given the difficulties in redistribution by selective centralization, it would seem reasonable to turn the solution around and adopt a program of general centralization of control on economic matters, with only selective decentralization. This solution is often what is meant by terms like central planning, centrally directed economy, or command economy. In a democratic form, a centrally directed economy would look something like this:

a. Resource allocation, growth, investment, distribution of incomes and wealth, prices, wages, and other crucial economic matters would be controlled by the decisions of a single Center, where overseers seek to develop and follow out a synoptic overview of desirable economic goals and instruments.

b. The Center itself would be democratically controlled by the demos.

There are elements of vagueness in the solution of redistribution by a centrally directed economy. These could be removed, if at all, only in an extended discussion. However, since our aim is not to examine either the solution in detail or its merits in general but to use it to explore the question of centralization, the phrasing may be exact enough.

Difficulties in redistribution by a centrally directed economy may be divided into two kinds: those having to do with part *a* and those having to do with part *b*. Some critics focus on *a*. Thus Lindblom argues that central or "synoptic" planning presupposes requirements that cannot be met. Synoptic planning would be possible.

(1) if the problem at hand does not go beyond man's cognitive capacities *and* (2) if there exist agreed criteria (rather than social conflict on values) by which solutions can be judged *and* (3) if the problem solvers have adequate incentives to stay with synoptical analysis until it is completed (rather than resort to rules of thumb, decision routines, guesstimates, and the like) (Lindblom 1977, 322).

He argues that none of these conditions is likely to be met, though "given emerging problems of nuclear weaponry, world order, environmental protection, and energy conservation, it may be that citizens and leaders all over the world will increasingly come to believe that we shall all live or die together." The chances that *all* three conditions will jointly obtain are so slim as to be negligible.

Adopting central direction simply puts a pretty facade on a ramshackle structure:

Hence, most ostensibly synoptic decision making is in fact accomplished by intuitive acts of judgment. . . . Or decisions are reached by the application of ideological guidelines, often inappropriate, if not actually foolish. Or by appeals to common sense, which bring both old prejudices and old insights to bear. Or by the invocation of moral principles, which on closer look would be disclosed as insufficient for the problem at hand. Or by reference to all manner of beliefs representing inherited prejudices, myths, misunderstandings, conventions, questionable rules of thumb, and the like, not excluding some serviceable insights. In any case, no synopsis (Lindblom 1977, 323).

If, however, central direction is intended to be not merely temporary but permanent, our interest here is less in part *a* than in part *b*. Is it likely that for the long run the overseers could be democratically controlled? Consider four problems. First, the solution both requires and helps to create an enormous concentration of political resources at the Center. A newspaper criticizes the government's conduct: curtail its supply of newsprint. A program malfunctions: doctor the data. A union supports the opposition party: hold back wage increases in the industry and make sure the union leaders get the message. A critic in parliament exposes these abuses: reduce allocations to the firms in his constituency. And so on. As with the usual abuses of authoritarian regimes it may be going too far to contend that these things are inevitable, but they are very likely.

To be sure, the institutional guarantees of polyarchy might be preserved in the beginning. Conceivably, codes of conduct for the overseers would develop or remain intact that would effectively prevent abuses of power. But if we assume that the overseers are not all that different from their predecessors, then abuse is likely. Perhaps in a democratic country where the political culture imposes much stronger restraints on political leaders than in the United States, the concentration of power required for redistribution by a centrally directed economy would not strengthen the authoritarian as against the democratic component in polyarchy. But surely in many countries the risk is great. One has only to reflect on what a Richard Nixon might accomplish in such a system. Under central direction the political resources potentially accessible to an unscrupulous executive and a small circle of close collaborators would far exceed even the most ambitious plans for insuring reelection and evening scores with enemies that were developed under Nixon's aegis.

The first difficulty suggests a second. Democratic control over the central planners depends heavily on the possibility of a coherent central plan. That is, the success of part *b* depends on the success of part *a*. It is one thing if the decisions of the overseers are made strictly according to a comprehensive plan that is discussed, enacted, and watched over by the legislature, the parties, the press, political associations, and the public. But it is quite another if such a plan is mainly facade and decisions are in fact made—and if Lindblom is right, must be made—by crude intuition, inappropriate ideological principles, prejudices, moral principles inadequate to the task, questionable rules of thumb, myths, and so on. For parliament to enact the plan and to supervise its execution would be exercises in futility far worse than the present struggles of legislative bodies to maintain effective control over executive programs, budgets, and revenues.

This leads us to the third consideration. The institutions of polyarchy that were developed to provide some measure of democratic control over the government of the state are poorly adapted to maintaining effective control over the kinds and volume of decisions that central direction envisions. Parliaments already find it notoriously difficult to exercise effective controls over complex executive and administrative organizations. If this is so with the more limited range of decisions that existing polyarchies seek to control, would the problem not be compounded by central direction?

The answer is suggested by the only experience similar to central direction that democratic countries have ever had: the wartime economies of Britain and the United States in the Second World War. In both countries, the institutions of polyarchy survived. In the United States, in fact, elections throughout the country continued on schedule, including the presidential election of 1944. Parliament and the Congress engaged in oversight, investigation, inquiry, criticism. In the United States Senate, the Truman committee not only made an obscure senator into a national figure but helped to expose and correct many of the abuses of the wartime bureaucracies. Questions of fairness in policies having an important impact on the distribution of benefits and obligations were aired in the House of Commons and the Congress, and the policies were sometimes changed by debate and votes in the national legislature. It seems reasonable to conclude that in both countries wartime planning worked well in achieving its purposes. The three necessary conditions suggested by Lindblom were pretty much met, for the overarching military objectives commanded more consensus in both countries than had ever existed or is likely to exist in peacetime, and they greatly simplified the task of determining basic priorities and the appropriate policies.

Even so, that task proved to be incredibly complex, and both Parliament and Congress, not to say the other institutions of democratic control, were at best only marginal in the main decisions made by the wartime agencies. Even with its highly developed system of committees and endless investigations, Congress could not exercise close surveillance over the myriad crucial decisions made by the wartime economic agencies (Young 1956, 225ff.). If the system had not been rapidly dismantled but had been allowed to exist indefinitely in peacetime, would institutions of popular control have increased their strength, or would democratic controls have been increasingly stifled by the enormous resources accessible to the chief executive?

But suppose popular controls *had* proved effective. Would they not have destroyed the synoptic (or pseudo-synoptic) aim of central decisions and produced instead a politicized economy where each major decision was a product of negotiation and bargaining among organized interests? This query suggests a fourth difficulty in the solution.

If the overseers do not free themselves from democratic controls, and if part *b* of the solution *is* satisfied, then synoptic planning would in all likelihood be impossible. As long as organizational pluralism and a plurality of interests continue to exist, and as long as interests are permitted to express themselves through the institutions of polyarchy, what reason is there to think that overseers at a single Center will be allowed to prepare and carry out a coherent set of economic policies designed in accordance with their overview of desirable economic goals and instruments? Unless there were a profound change in civic orientations—and we have not assumed such a change—would not "politics" tend to fragment any such single overview?

Let us imagine that an industry—shipbuilding, for example— could no longer survive without subsidies. New technologies, changes in demand, rising costs, excess capacity left over from a previous period of expansion, all make it reasonable to shift labor and capital out of the industry. Although the overseers, let us suppose, try to ease the process with transitional subsidies to industry and workers, they adhere to their goal of reducing employment and production in the industry. Will workers, families, neighbors, local merchants, managers, and other affected interests necessarily share the view of the overseers as to the reasonableness of the policy? Experience suggests that the injured groups might well think it highly reasonable to ask for greater subsidies over a longer, perhaps an indefinite period and that their political spokesmen would echo or amplify these demands. Unless there were substantial change in civic orientations or in political institutions, or both, might the representatives of the injured groups not negotiate a change in the overall plan? Changes would take place not merely in one industry but in a dozen or a hundred parts of the overseers' tidy framework of policies. If so, the synoptic framework would be no more than a bundle of sticks.

Thus centralized direction harbors an internal conflict between part *a* and part *b*: If the overseers at the Center have sufficient power, resources, and autonomy in relation to other subsystems to develop and carry out policies reflecting their overview of economic goals and instruments, then they probably cannot be indefinitely subject to effective democratic control. If, on the other hand, they *are* subject to a high degree of democratic control by means of the institutions of polyarchy, then they cannot have sufficient power, resources, and autonomy to develop and carry out their overview.

Would it be different if the economy were publicly rather than privately owned? Unless public ownership were accompanied by a much more extensive transformation in civic orientations than a simple belief in the desirability of public as against private ownership, it is hard to see why the internal conflict between the two parts of the solution would be reduced. To be sure, since no democratic country has ever tried state socialism (or extensive social ownership in any form) we lack the crucial experiment. Experience with state socialism in the authoritarian regimes of the Soviet Union and Eastern Europe is, strictly speaking, not decisive; but that experience is hardly encouraging.

It is significant that the occasional dissenters speaking out for democratic socialism in these countries usually advocate greater decentralization of economic control. And humanist Marxists tend to insist, as in Yugoslavia, on the crucial importance of decentralization. So far as one can tell from fragments of evidence in countries where the overseers have had the greatest opportunities to show the benefits of a centrally directed economy, democratic and humanist dissenters, who know these systems from the inside, strongly support decentralization.

Would a form of socialism that was both decentralized and democratic provide an answer more promising than either selective centralization or a centrally directed economy?

Decentralized Democratic Socialism

Pre-Marxist socialists, the Utopians so scathingly condemned by Marx and Engels, mainly envisioned socialist orders consisting of relatively autonomous economic enterprises or communities. Although Marx's own writings can be read to support both centralization and decentralization, the main thrust of socialist thought after Marx was strongly centralist. For generations, most socialists believed that a socialist economic order would operate more or less as a centrally directed economy. Both orthodox Marxists like the leaders of the German Social Democratic party and non-Marxist socialists like the Fabians in Britain agreed that socialism required a fairly high degree of central direction. Although the older decentralist current was kept alive (more often by anarchists and syndicalists than by democratic socialists), it drifted out of the main stream. The construction of the modern world's first socialist regime in the Soviet Union and the political and ideological preeminence of Soviet Communism over other socialist currents further strengthened the centralist thrust of socialist ideas. Even Stalinism did not, at first, destroy confidence in the centralist vision. For however much democratic socialists loathed Stalinism as a political system, many held that the centrally directed economy of the Soviet Union revealed how a socialist economy ought to be organized; the vision of many democratic socialists was, in substance, a Soviet economy in a democratic political order.

In recent years, socialist faith in centralization has waned. For one thing, the oppressiveness of authoritarian socialism in the Soviet Union and other state socialist countries stimulated doubts about the desirability or even the possibility of achieving democratic socialism with centralized controls. Yugoslavia's break with the Soviet Union and its turn toward a highly decentralized socialist economy also awakened socialists to the possibilities of a decentralized economic order. Though Yugoslavia lacks some of the crucial institutions of polyarchy and is hardly as democratic in its political institutions as democratic socialists would like, the idea and institutions of self-management appealed to humanistic Marxists and democratic socialists throughout the world. Experiences with centralized controls in nonsocialist countries governed by polyarchy also led to disappointment with centralization, a disappointment all the sharper because many of the centralized controls in these countries were a product of reforms that labor and socialist parties themselves had advocated. As a result of influences like these, an important shift took place in socialist thinking. Where the main thrust of socialist ideas had been centralist for generations, democratic socialists now began to look favorably on ideas for decentralizing controls to relatively autonomous enterprises and other subsystems.

Thus democratic socialism once again shares an important part of the vision, though not the specific ideas, of many pre-Marxist Utopian socialists. It is fair to say that today most democratic socialists are pluralists, if not explicitly at least by implication. It is important, therefore, to explore the question whether a decentralized socialist order along the following lines would manage to escape the problems of organizational pluralism or the limits set by the fundamental dilemmas:

a. Decisions on output, purchases, resource allocation within enterprises, products, prices, wages, distribution of earnings, loans, investment in equipment, and so on would be (mainly) made by the governments of enterprises.

b. Though mainly autonomous on these matters, enterprises would be subject to the general laws and policies of the government of the state.

c. The government of the state would be democratically controlled.

Needless to say, this sketch of decentralized democratic socialism is vague about crucial issues. Not only are there the usual problems of describing a solution to a highly complex question in a few words, but the vagueness of the sketch also reflects some controversies as to how the enterprises are supposed to function. Because an adequate discussion of these issues would take us beyond the focus of this book, I will deal summarily with a complex set of questions.

Two questions are particularly critical. Are the enterprises to operate competitively within a market system or not? And how are they to be managed or governed? Historically, Marxists and non-Marxist socialists were often strongly hostile to the idea of a market economy, which was closely associated with the structures, culture, and civic orientations of capitalism. It seemed all but self-evident that socialism must destroy the anarchy of the market, the mystification of prices, the evils inherent in competition. Yet no satisfactory way has been discovered, either in theory or in practice, for eliminating markets and at the same time allowing enterprises a substantial degree of autonomy. Theory and historical experiences argue strongly that a system of enterprises governed *neither* by the market *nor* by central planners would run headlong into chaos.

A second ambiguity in the sketch arises from disagreements among socialists on how economic enterprises should be governed. Should they be run exclusively by the workers in the particular enterprise (in large enterprises by their elected representatives) or should other affected interests, such as consumers, suppliers, or the general public, have a direct voice in enterprise governments?

TABLE 6. Four Versions of Decentralized Socialism

| | | Market economy: | |
		Yes	No
Workers' control	Yes	(a)	(b)
	No	(c)	(d)

(Though only a professional economist is likely to find the proposal at all attractive, it might even be technically possible for managers appointed by the central government to operate publicly owned enterprises strictly according to the requirements of a competitive price system.)

Some of the options for decentralized socialism are suggested by table 6. Although democratic socialists are very far from agreed on which of these is the best approach, the most coherent and rigorous body of socialist theory today recommends a, that is, market socialism with workers' control (e.g. Vanek 1970, and Schweikart 1980). A long-standing socialist commitment to industrial democracy, close and critical scrutiny of the Soviet economy, the example of Yugoslavia, and the influence of post-Marxist economic analysis on a number of socialist economists all helped to increase interest among democratic socialists in the possibilities of combining market socialism with self-managed or worker-controlled enterprises. However, although this vision of decentralized socialism has become influential among socialists, it has by no means won their general approbation. The older visions of either a centrally planned economic order or decentralization achieved somehow without markets still retain a good deal of support.

In any case, no proposal for decentralized democratic socialism can altogether escape the problems of pluralism or the dilemmas that limit solutions to these problems (cf. Rusinow 1977, 245–307, 345). For example, in any system of autonomous enterprises, differences in enterprise incomes are sure to spring up because of differences in internal efficiencies, the skills of workers and managers, accessibility to and relations with suppliers and consumers, the age and quality of equipment, consumers' choices and demands, decisions as to how enterprise earnings are to be allocated between wages, bonuses, social services, depreciation, and investment in new capital equipment, and so on. Unless some invisible hand works toward redistribution, the workers in some enterprises will enjoy significantly higher incomes than others. Inequalities arising from these causes are independent of, and likely to be amplified by, inequalities brought about because of tendencies toward oligarchy and status, which as we suggested in chapter 3 would surely exist within the enterprise itself. The inequalities arising from various causes might be reduced to justifiable levels if (1) because of a profound and widespread change in civic orientations, workers in more prosperous enterprises voluntarily transfer some of their income to workers in the less profitable enterprises, or (2) in the absence of voluntary tranfers, the enterprises lose some of their autonomy to decision makers at the Center, who enforce certain uniformities on all enterprises. Both possibilities violate our assumptions. To the extent that (2) holds and (1) does not, then decentralized democratic socialism would face many of the same difficulties as redistribution by selective centralization.

Or consider the question of protecting broader interests—the general good, the public interest, the interests of the working class as a whole—and so on. Is there much reason to suppose that workers in autonomous enterprises would spontaneously seek to maximize broader interests as against their own particularistic interests? Are we to expect some kind of hidden hand at work in a decentralized socialist economy that will cause group egoism to converge somehow on the good of all? Presumably the hidden hand in market socialism would be what it is supposed to be in market capitalism: competition among firms in the market. But in market capitalism, competition among firms cannot be maintained or undesirable externalities reduced without regulation by the central government. Yet without a major transformation in civic orientations, would not many of the same political difficulties in regulating firms in a capitalist order also arise in a *democratic* socialist order?

Any search for solutions to problems like these must necessarily confront the familiar dilemmas. Thus if we grant that workers have a moral right to participate in governing the enterprises in which they work, does their right transcend all utilitarian considerations of efficiency? One might reply that there is no conflict between participation and efficiency, that workers' control would not reduce and might actually increase efficiency; or that in a system of self-governing enterprises the greater satisfaction, well-being, self-respect, and happiness of workers would outweigh any likely losses in consumer satisfaction, even on a strict but more comprehensive utilitarian calculation; or that if the gains in the well-being of citizens as producers do not fully match their losses as consumers, the right of self-government in enterprises is intrinsically so desirable, or forms such an integral network with the rights to self-government in the larger domain of the state, that these rights ought not be overridden by a concern for material well-being. However, would it be unreasonable if workers, acting in their role as citizens and fully exercising their democratic rights, were to reduce their own rights as workers in governing the enterprises in order to strengthen the efficiency of enterprises and their own rights as consumers? I do not mean to suggest answers to these questions but only to show that a proposal for decentralized democratic socialism must immediately confront the dilemmas inherent in large-scale democracy.

Consider another dilemma. Grant that workers ought to govern their own lives. But which workers on what questions? What is a rightful demos on what range of issues? What constitutes an "enterprise" for purposes of autonomous self-government? What demos is to decide *this* question? And when the "enterprise" has been defined, what is the proper demos *within* an enterprise?

Let one issue serve to show the force of the dilemma. Should part-time or seasonal workers have the same rights as permanent workers in an enterprise? It might be argued that temporary workers, like temporary residents of a country, ought not to have the same rights of citizenship as the regular workers. When the Peruvian military regime inaugurated a system of workers' control in the

Peruvian sugar industry, the members (*socios*) were defined as the full-time, regular, nonseasonal workers. Only *socios* were entitled to participate in governing the enterprises and thus to determine the distribution of earnings. Like the previous corporately owned industry, the worker-controlled cooperatives hired seasonal day laborers (*rentados* or *eventuales*) to cut the cane. The day laborers were not *socios*. Already a privileged stratum of skilled workers within the Peruvian population, the *socios* now had a collective interest in limiting their own numbers in order to increase each member's share of the earnings. Thus the *socios* had a direct conflict of interest with the nonmembers. To reduce the privileges of the *socios* required intervention by the central government. But the skilled sugar workers were also the main clients of the military leadership that had brought about the revolution and inaugurated workers' control. Was the regime to antagonize its own supporters in order to benefit the day laborers, a politically much less weighty group? (Stepan 1978, 216ff.).

Probably few democratic socialists would quarrel with the notion that decentralized socialism would require some centralization and concentration. To maintain general norms of distributive justice in a decentralized economy, whether socially owned or private and whether market or nonmarket oriented, would require a Center with a concentration of resources sufficient to enable it to ensure that those norms were uniformly maintained. How much centralization and concentration would be required? Would not the structure of self-management itself—the constitutional system, so to speak, of the democratically controlled enterprises—have to be brought about and enforced by the central government? If so, does that not imply a very powerful Center indeed? It is significant that in Yugoslavia self-management was brought about by an authoritarian regime, and the subsequent changes in norms and structures have been carried through largely by the central government. As we have just noted, the system of workers' control in Peru was instituted and enforced by military dictatorship. Important as they are, these cases do not compel the conclusion that only an authoritarian regime can force workers to be free. But it is hard to see how a general and more or less uniform structure of decentralized democratic socialism could be inaugurated or maintained without a considerable degree of centralization and concentration.

The Limits of Structural Change

As we have seen in discussing the various solutions sketched in this chapter, the extent to which structural changes can achieve their ostensible purposes is severely limited by the civic orientations of citizens and leaders. To understand more clearly why a change in structures is unlikely by itself to produce satisfactory solutions to the problem of democratic pluralism, let me return to the question of the distribution of income. The more that overseers at the Center control the distribution of income (and, of course, wealth), as in a centrally directed economy, the more the distribution will depend on the civic orientations of the overseers. But even if a regime were fully democratic and the economy were socially owned, unless great changes in civic consciousness were also to occur, significant inequalities in income might exist. Indeed, the more democratic a regime, the less the distribution of income depends on economic structures and the more it depends on civic consciousness.

To see why this is so, let us imagine a country in which the government satisfies all the criteria of democracy set out earlier and where collective decisions are made strictly according to the principle of majority rule. To begin with, let the economy be privately owned and the distribution of income highly unequal. We shall also suppose that civic orientations induce all citizens to act as rational egoists who always seek their own economic advantage. Conceivably, a majority of rational egoists in a perfectly democratic system would progressively change incomes at both ends of the distribution in order to arrive at a more egalitarian distribution of income. However, as I suggested earlier, rational egoists might also form majorities to support any one of an indefinite number of possible distributions: While the lower- and middle-income groups might form a coalition against the top, the middle and upper might also unite against the lower, or the lower and upper against the middle, and so on. Moreover, no outcome would necessarily be stable, since some persons could always gain by a new redistributive coalition. Unless civic orientations were more egalitarian and benevolent than we have just postulated, there is no reason why a majority of citizens would endorse economic equality rather than inequality.

It might be argued that in a country with a capitalist economic system, only a very limited range of distributions is possible, and all of them must necessarily be inegalitarian. Conceivably this may be so. But the strictly necessary connections between capitalism and income distribution are far more tenuous than is often assumed. What pattern of income distribution would a majority of citizens who were rational but not necessarily egoistic choose, having already accepted as given the structure of private enterprise and a market economy? It was once argued by some neoclassical economists that if all resources of land, labor, and capital were priced in a competitive market, and if enterprises were run for profit, then incomes would be allocated in direct proportion to the value of each person's product (Clark 1902). Thus capitalism would achieve the goal that Marx once offered for socialism in its initial stage: from each according to ability, to each according to social contribution. Presumably, then, a rational demos would leave income allocation to the market and prevent the government from engaging in any redistribution. Few if any economists would defend such a preposterous notion today. In recent years, economists have generally acknowledged that it is beyond their capacities as economic theorists to specify what constitutes a just or proper distribution of income. Their theorizing simply takes the distribution of incomes as a given, and not a matter they can specify, at least as professional economists. But if the distribution of incomes is itself unjust, then all the theoretical marvels of modern economics cannot undo the injustice. Like a slave society of great elegance and refinement, a society in which the distribution of income is unjust is still . . . unjust.

In a private-enterprise, market-oriented economy, the proper distribution of income is not primarily a technical question but a political and moral question. How is the question to be decided? To let the market allocate incomes requires, at least implicitly, a collective decision and a judgment about the moral qualities of that distribution. A decision to go in the other direction and choose equality on the ground that it maximizes want satisfaction is also not merely technical; it too is political and moral. Suppose, for example, that the citizens are not simple utilitarians, are not benevolent, or believe in certain absolute rights to the income from "their" property?

Because the distribution of income requires some sort of collective decision, if only to insist that the government must stand aside and let the market work its effects; because a reasonable decision requires empirical judgments (often highly complex) as to the relative likelihood of different consequences; and because a decision is also inescapably a moral judgment, there appears to be enough ground to support claims to an indefinite number of different principles. Here is a sample:

a. Incomes are to be allocated exclusively by the market.
b. Departures from the market allocation are permitted only if no one is made worse off.
c. To each according to the value of the social product contributed by each.
d. To each according to the value of the work each performs.
e. To each according to the amount, duration, and intensity of work each performs (Marx 1974b, 346).
f. No increase in the inequality of a distribution is permissible:
    f.1. Unless the worst off are not made worse off by the change.
    f.2. Unless the worst off are made better off by the change.
g. Personal incomes are to be distributed equally unless an unequal distribution is to everyone's advantage (Rawls 1971, 62).
h. Choose only those augmentations of inequality that advantage some strata and disadvantage none. (Rae 1979, 149).
i. Income of the top quintile should not be more than:

i.1. Five times the income of the bottom quintile (Thurow 1980, 202).

i.2. Four times the bottom quintile (de Lone 1979, 197).

j. From each according to his or her ability, to each according to his or her needs (Marx 1974b, 347).

k. Personal incomes are to be allocated equally to families.

l. Personal incomes are to be allocated equally to individuals.

It might be objected that some of these possibilities are inconsistent with a privately owned economy—for example, because of effects on incentives to invest or to work. But do major inconsistencies arise primarily because of effects on incentives or instead because of civic orientations in countries with privately owned economies? If the latter, surely these civic orientations are not wholly incapable of change. If they could change enough to support social ownership, could they not change enough to support much greater income equality without social ownership? If socialism requires both social ownership and greater equalization of incomes, then the change in civic orientations needed to achieve socialism looks to be considerably greater than the change required to achieve greater income equalization within a privately owned system. If the change in civic orientations required for socialism were attainable, would not the other change be more easily attainable?

I am not about to suggest answers to these questions. However, in order to eliminate the issue of the limits set by private ownership, suppose we assume that enterprises are publicly or socially owned. We need not specify exactly the processes for allocating incomes and determining the shape of the distribution: Perhaps personal incomes would result simply from the initial distribution of enterprise income, or, as in capitalist countries, from the effects of taxes and transfer payments on this initial distribution, or from a combination of the two, or from other unspecified processes.

Are not all the distributive principles that are listed above, as well as many others, equally consistent with social ownership? In describing the distributive principles of socialism, Marxists often advance the conjecture Marx made in his brief criticism of the program enacted at the Gotha Congress in 1875 at which the two German socialist parties were united, that is, *e* followed in the fullness of time by *j*. But why *would* or *should* a socialist country adopt *e* rather than the others? And why would or should *j* finally displace *e*? Marx nowhere set out compelling reasons; and with rather less creative and critical spirit than Marx himself displayed, Marxists often treat these principles as self-evident. But none of the distributive principles in our sample list is at all self-evident. And surely none should be accepted without question as a principle of distribution that the demos in a democratic socialist country either would or should adopt.

A given structure, then, could be accompanied by many different kinds of civic orientations. What is achieved by a structural change will therefore depend on the civic orientations associated with that change. No structural change, though accompanied by the minimal changes in civic consciousness required to bring it about, appears to be sufficient to overcome all the disadvantages of democratic pluralism or to escape the fundamental dilemmas inherent in large-scale democracy itself.

7

Changing Civic Orientations

Is it possible for citizens in a democratic country to conduct themselves in their public affairs so that the interests of each are harmonious with the interests of all?

Those who attribute to organizational pluralism a major responsibility for deforming civic consciousness seem to imply that the seeds of a widespread commitment to a public or collective good lie buried beneath the arid surface of civic consciousness, awaiting only the proper cultivation to spring forth like desert flowers after a rain. Recommendations for cultivating public spirit sometimes appear to presume that nothing more is needed than exhortation. Frequently, however, solutions presuppose a structural change of some sort—democratization, central planning, decentralization, collective ownership, and so on. Yet as we have seen, structural changes like these cannot guarantee social harmony or civic virtue. Moreover, a difficulty with all structural solutions, as we saw in the last chapter, is that structures and consciousness are loosely coupled. Neither capitalist nor socialist economic structures, it appears, have brought about the civic orientations their advocates would like, and certainly neither has achieved social harmony.

Nevertheless, social structures and civic consciousness do influence one another. To what extent, then, must democratic pluralism necessarily weaken civic virtue by fostering egoism and political conflict? No question in this book is more densely packed with booby traps. The question touches on complex issues surrounding the very meaning and ground of terms like *public, virtue, good, interest, good of all,* and so on; unsolved problems of how individual choices, interests, preferences, or goods can be aggregated into a justifiable collective decision, as in the voters' paradox and Arrow's impossibility theorem;* and issues of a general kind confronting democracy, such as the controversy over justifications for the majority principle. Difficulties are compounded by the absence of a common universe of discourse; relevant discussions are carried on in fundamentally different language-games, to use Wittgenstein's term. For example, how if at all should we distinguish between a person's interests, good, and welfare? (Barry 1965, 173–206). Moreover, philosophers and social theorists who propose routes to greater civic virtue often neglect to cast their ideas in concepts suitable for determining precisely what they assume about individual behavior or consciousness, or how, concretely, civic virtue is to be brought about. Finally, the understanding *of* human consciousness *by* human consciousness is too feeble to support confident statements about absolute limits on the future development of human consciousness.

Because I cannot possibly do justice to issues like these in this brief book, I propose to set them brutally aside, on the assumption that it may still be possible to discuss fruitfully one question that is particularly germane to the problem of democratic pluralism: In what way are civic orientations toward the public good affected by the *scale* of political life in a system as large as a country, or larger? Democratic pluralism reflects, after all, a special application of democratic ideas. It is a product of the attempt—historically speaking

---

*The voters' paradox, first shown by Condorcet in the eighteenth century, is produced by the fact that, given certain not unlikely distributions of voters' preferences among three or more alternatives, a majority exists for *each* of the alternatives and thus no rational collective choice is possible (Frohlich and Oppenheimer 1978, 16–19). In 1951 Kenneth J. Arrow elaborated the voters' paradox into a stunning demonstration that, given a few reasonable assumptions, any collective choice would either have to be imposed with no regard at all to the preferences of the members of a group, or would be determined by only one member, i.e., a dictator (Arrow 1951; MacKay 1980).

quite recent—to apply democratic processes not on the small scale of a village or a city-state but on the large scale of a modern country. As we shall see in a moment, its distinctive features—the large scale of the demos, the institutions of polyarchy, the existence of many relatively autonomous subsystems—may make certain kinds of civic orientations unlikely, perhaps even impossible to develop. Yet proposals for solving the problem of democratic pluralism, and particularly for overcoming deformations in civic consciousness, frequently ignore the differences between what may be theoretically possible in a small-scale democracy and what may be impossible, as a practical matter, in a large-scale democracy.

Part of the recurring appeal of Rousseau and the Greek ideal of the city-state on which he drew is a vision that offers hope of satisfying the unquenchable longing for life in a solidary and self-sufficient community: harmonious, total, monistic, where kinship and friendship blend with citizenship, where work, economic life, recreation, politics, the life of the mind and spirit, all exist in the same familiar social, political, and territorial space—the neighborhood, commune, village, town, city. This is a vision of the democratized gemeinschaft—as it never was, and probably never can be.

From classical Greece to Rousseau, the assumption that the community would be small both in area and in numbers of citizens decisively influenced not only democratic theory but also thinking about civic virtue and the common good. On the smaller scale of the little community, interdependence was palpable, the community sharply defined, the commonalities often rather apparent. Although towns and cities were frequently torn asunder by internal strife and faction, not to mention wars between one city and another, the idea of a common good transcending factional interests and conflicts would have been easily understood. It was plausible and natural to think of one's community as an extension of one's family and circle of friends. A village might literally be so. No doubt many communities, often perhaps under the threat or in the wake of common disaster, gave concrete evidence of a precious solidarity, of common purposes which everyone in the community shared and which they might cooperate to attain.

In nineteenth-century Europe the visible displacement of gemeinschaft by gesellschaft, in Tönnies's memorable formulation (Tönnies [1887] 1957), helped to create in many intellectual circles a nostalgia for the solidary community that once had existed, somewhere, and was now lost. The idealization of the Greek polis touched a surprising variety of important thinkers. Marx, here too deeply influenced by Hegel, seems to have shared the vision of the idealized polis in which citizens, for the last time in history, had been whole and unalienated. In England the extraordinary influence of classical studies lent historical concreteness to the idea of a polity with an overarching common good that citizens could apprehend and should strive to attain (Turner 1981, 213–34). This view is strongly echoed in Mill's insistence in *Representative Government* on reducing the electoral weight of, or in the extreme cases excluding from the suffrage, those who would be most likely to place their own class interests ahead of the common good—mainly, in his view, the very poor and uneducated (Mill 1947, 212–22). Mill's notion of citizenship was essentially Greek; yet the English polity was no tiny polis where knowledge of the common good might require little more than the direct and a-theoretical experience of community life. It was instead a nation-state, where the commonalities of fundamental interest were far more problematical. Thus like democracy itself, a conception of the common good that may have been weak in specifics but had some meaning in the context of a small community was transferred to the vastly larger scale of the nation-state. This displacement of the idea of the common good from the small city to the enormous nation-state generally took place with little explicit concern for the possibility that such a large change in scale might radically alter the meaning and applicability of concepts like the common good, the general interest, the good of all, the community, civic virtue, and so on.

Yet this change in scale has radical consequences for the possibilities of conscious cooperation to achieve a common good, and it is those I intend to explore in this chapter.

The Quest for Civic Virtue

Civic virtue may be said to exist among some aggregate of persons if each person involved in making collective decisions (hence in a democratic system, all citizens) acts steadily on the conscious intention of achieving the good of all the persons in the aggregate. Either conflicts of interest do not arise; or, if they do, citizens give priority to the public good. Although this definition of civic virtue is loose, it will serve.

Civic virtue so defined might depend in turn on several different kinds of orientations, which I am going to call individualist, moral, and organic. Although these orientations could coexist among different citizens or operate within the same citizen at different times, it is helpful to consider them separately.

Individualist Civic Virtue

Imagine a community in which citizens see themselves as distinct and morally autonomous persons (as contrasted with what I shall describe in a moment as a community with organic civic virtue). Because in this community all citizens are latent egoists, a citizen who perceived a conflict between his own good and that of the community would choose his own good. But civic harmony exists precisely because little or no conflict of interests is perceived to exist. Citizens perceive their interests in such a way that in choosing what is best for oneself in collective matters, each necessarily also chooses the good of all. Conversely, in choosing the common good in collective decisions, each necessarily chooses what is best for oneself. This is essentially the solution to the problem of civic virtue that Rousseau offers in the *Social Contract*, the *Geneva Manuscript*, and the *Essay on Political Economy* (Rousseau 1978, 62–63, 175, 218–19).

Unlike some prescriptions for civic virtue, the assumption of individualism makes only modest demands on human character but exceptionally strong demands on the structure of society. It does not require citizens to act altruistically or from a sense of moral obligation so powerful as to override self-interest. Yet if it deals lightly with citizens in these respects, it does require at last two conditions not so easy to achieve. Obviously citizens must perceive that their interests are fundamentally harmonious. And if the perceptions are to be in some sense correctly grounded in reality (thus not specious, not entirely a product of "false consciousness"), then the interests of different citizens must all be harmonious in some reasonably objective sense.

I suggested earlier that the city-states of Greece and medieval Italy seem to have fallen well short of meeting these two requirements. Striving for and agreeing on a common good manifested itself far more as an ideal than as a steady and dominant orientation that actually determined the conduct of citizens. It is imaginable, nonetheless, that these two requirements *could* be met in a small and quite homogeneous community. But is it conceivable that they could be met on the scale of a country or any equally large aggregate of persons? If small size is a necessary requirement for a citizen body sufficiently homogeneous to prevent conflicts of interest, then a necessary but not sufficient condition for individualist civic virtue is that the polity must be small. With increasing size in both population and territory, two crucial changes are sure to take place, both of which drastically reduce the prospects for individualist civic virtue. These are an increase in (1) diversity of interests and (2) the need for theoretical rather than practical knowledge to determine the common good in concrete situations.

1. The larger a collectivity, the more likely it is to contain both subjective and objective diversities. A unit as large as a country is certain to include a great many diversities of both kinds. Although actual patterns vary a good deal in different countries, it is difficult to see how political life in a modern country could avoid many of the kinds of conflicts described in chapter 4, except by removing the institutional guarantees that allow the various cleavages to be orga-

nized and the conflicts publicly expressed, that is, by suppressing the democratic components of polyarchy. Even in countries much smaller and far more homogeneous than the United States, like Denmark, diversity guarantees the existence of political conflicts. Moreover, as we have seen, there is no convincing reason why replacing private with public ownership would cause political conflicts among individuals and groups to disappear. If one reflects on the issues discussed in previous chapters—democratization, centralization, decentralization, income distribution, ownership, workers' control—no solution would be so obviously beneficial to everyone in a socialist order as to eradicate conflicts of interest and insure political harmony.

2. Moreover, as the number of persons increases, knowledge of the public good necessarily becomes more theoretical and less practical. It becomes more and more difficult for any citizen to know all the other citizens concretely. Beyond some limit—a limit that on the scale of a country (let alone humanity) is infinitesimally small—concrete knowledge of the others is flatly impossible. Beyond infinitesimally small limits, then, the "community" is no longer a body of concrete human beings actually known to one another, much less an association of friends; it is an aggregate of distant persons called class, nation, country, humanity, or what not. How is a citizen to apprehend the interests of the people who comprise aggregates like these? The good of the aggregate must now be interpreted by means of abstractions that may form at one extreme an elaborate philosophical or social theory and at the other nothing more than the naive assumption that all the other members of the aggregate have interests identical with oneself. It follows that as the number of persons in the aggregate increases, valid knowledge of what the common interest or the general good might be in specific situations must necessarily depend less and less on one's own direct experiences and perceptions of others, and more and more on images and abstractions. If knowledge of the common interest becomes more theoretical than practical, does civic virtue require that all citizens be highly proficient theorists? If citizens should prove to be inade-

quate theorists, and it is reasonable to expect they would be, must we conclude with Plato that government by citizens is inherently inferior to government by guardians who are theoretically more adept? Finally, given the persistence throughout history of conflict over philosophical and ideological views, is there much reason for believing that either philosopher-citizens or philosopher-kings would actually agree on a unique solution for every problem requiring a collective decision?

Moral Civic Virtue

One reason for the extreme vulnerability of individualist civic virtue is that, by assumption, citizens are latent egoists. Consequently, whenever a citizen perceives a conflict between his own interests and the general good, he naturally chooses to advance his own interests. Such a fragile foundation has not usually been thought sufficient to sustain virtue, whether private or public. An alternative assumption is that in all their collective decisions citizens would be animated by a moral orientation. By a moral orientation I mean that a citizen believes the good or interest of every person (or at least every person in the specific collectivity, whether city-state, nation-state, class, or whatever) is entitled to equal weight and consideration; and this belief is so powerful that when one engages in collective decisions, one intends and acts to achieve the just alternative rather than one's own interests, even when the just alternative conflicts with one's own interests. A moral orientation might also be called a commitment to justice.

Does a moral orientation—a commitment to justice—provide a stronger foundation for civic virtue than an individualist orientation? Where individualism exists, civic virtue prevails only as long as citizens can aim simultaneously at their own good and the community good; it vanishes whenever the two targets diverge. By contrast, where moral orientations prevail, the targets need not be identical, for when they diverge, each citizen continues to aim at the good of the community rather than his own. The problem, of course, is how to bring about and sustain strong moral orientations among a large aggregate of persons. Once again as an aggregate increases in size, the problem grows more acute because of increasing strains on (1) the moral commitment itself; (2) the affective support for it; and (3) the cognitive requirements for apprehending the public good in specific cases.

1. As diversities show up, cleavages develop, and political conflicts appear, differences between the general good and the perceived interests of oneself or one's group become an increasingly common feature of political life. Thus one's egoistic interests constantly hammer away at one's commitment to the public good.

Moreover, with increasing scale a moral orientation toward justice undergoes a critical transformation. If justice means that the interests of each person are to be given equal weight and consideration, then in a small group one can assume that one's own interests will be well considered, just as the interests of each of the others will also be well considered. But the weight that can be justly assigned to one's own interests necessarily diminishes in direct proportion to the number of persons in a collectivity. Among, say, a million people the weight that principles of justice would assign to one's own interests in a collective decision becomes so minuscule that for all practical purposes it vanishes. If we define altruism as giving priority to the good of other persons over one's own, then the larger the scale of the collectivity the more that a commitment to justice requires altruism. Are we to conclude, then, that in a large system civic virtue requires citizens to be steadily altruistic in public affairs? If so, what emotions and motivations can possibly be strong enough to sustain civic virtue?

2. Although writers who prescribe civic virtue are often vague in revealing exactly how principles of justice are to be integrated into a person's character, emotions, and actions, from Aristotle onward they have frequently supposed that a predisposition for acting justly toward others could be adequately supported by strong habits and ties of love, affection, friendship, neighborliness, fellow feeling, sympathy, and the like. Given sufficiently powerful feelings like these, justice blends imperceptibly with egoism and may be sus-

tained even if one's egoistic interests occasionally take a few hard knocks. What is remarkable about these affective bonds, however, is how much they depend on intimacy and direct relationships. As the number of others increases, love, friendship, neighborliness, and so on are necessarily transformed into something quite different. To love a member of one's family or a friend is not at all like "loving" abstract "others" whom one does not know, never expects to know, and may not even want to know.

True, people sometimes acquire loyalties to abstract aggregates like "country," and some people profess to "love humanity." Although emotions and identifications like these may buttress altruism and moral commitments for some people, and may on occasion call forth sacrifices from a large number of citizens, the experience of the species shows them to be poor competitors in a steady, flat-out contest with individual and group egoism. Without gainsaying the possibility that some persons may sometimes act out of genuine benevolence or altruism toward the interests of large aggregates of persons whom they cannot possibly know as individuals, actual cases are rarer than conventional views admit. It is often said of one who dies in battle that he died out of love for his country. But studies of American and German soldiers in World War II confirm what soldiers have doubtless always known. Morale, combat efficiency, and the willingness to make sacrifices depend greatly on relations within the small group. One is less likely to die for one's country, it seems, than for one's buddies (Shils 1951, 64).

If the affective support for justice and altruism that might exist in small and closely bonded groups grows too weak to sustain civic virtue among a large aggregate of people, on what is civic virtue to depend? Some moral philosophers, like Kant, appear to have pinned their hopes on reason. But is unaided reason sufficient to overcome the powerful thrust of egoistic strivings? Experience suggests that with many of us reason is often the servant and not the master of egoism.

3. As we have seen, reasoning about the public good grows difficult with an increase in the number of persons. Precisely as in a

polity where civic virtue is based on individualism, so also where civic virtue is based on moral orientations, with increasing scale the task of correctly apprehending the public good must necessarily come to depend less and less on direct experience and practical understanding and more and more on theoretical reasoning. Prescriptions for both moral and individualist civic virtue in a large-scale polity thus confront the same dilemma. If the regime is to be democratic, one cannot reasonably expect civic virtue to prevail as a steady orientation; and if civic virtue is steadily to prevail in collective decisions, the regime cannot, it seems, be democratic. The path traced out of this dilemma by the argument for guardianship is as ancient as Plato and well marked. But actual experience with government by self-chosen guardians, particularly in this century, indicates that the path often leads straight through the gates of a vast prison camp.

Organic Civic Virtue
A third route would require human identity to expand beyond the individual to a collectivity. The psychophysical processes by which this transformation is to be accomplished are not at all clear. Rousseau briefly alluded to it in a draft of the *Geneva Manuscript* but, in order to show its impossibility, spoke of the need for a kind of central nervous system uniting different persons (Rousseau 1978, 159). Perhaps the idea is best illustrated with a fanciful example from Marcel Aymé's ironic story *Les Sabines*. A beautiful woman, Sabine, has the capacity to duplicate herself—to create a perfect clone, we might say today. The twin sisters retain a single psyche, so that each participates fully in all the experiences of the other. Since the twins cannot resist the temptation to clone themselves, the sisterhood expands more or less geometrically, growing to some 67,000. Despite occasional confusions and mishaps, initially their collective life is deliriously exhilarating. Yet because each feels not only the joys of the others but also the acute misery of one sister who is subjected to terrifying abuse, the burden of collective selfhood grows heavy and the common suffering becomes almost unbearable.

A less fantastic account, more in keeping with the limits of human physiology, might be described like this: The boundaries that Alpha perceives to separate her from Beta grow fainter; Alpha's personal identity—let me call it her *individual* self—expands to incorporate Beta's wants, joys, and pains; Alpha's "I" and "mine" recede and are replaced by "we" and "ours." Thus Alpha's individual self is transformed into a *collective* self, in which Beta's interests are no longer distinguishable from her own. The image that comes most readily to mind is mother and infant: when the child suffers, the mother suffers, as if the child's suffering were her own, which in a sense it is. Some of Marx's writing, particularly his early work, is open to an interpretation roughly along these lines (cf. Kolakowski 1978, 1:162, 363). Thus Ollman describes how, according to Marx, in a communist society "a person can no longer satisfy his own need by depriving others, since the effect of their disappointment would punish him along with everyone else." To this extent communist man represents the perfect intersection of one's own needs with the interests of others that characterizes individualist civic virtue. Ollman goes on to say, however, that

In harness with this belief, both affecting it and being affected by it, is communist man's conception of others and their necessary objects as extensions of himself. . . . Through this conceptual revolution, the individual has, in effect, supplied himself with a new subject, the community, for all but his most personal activities. . . . With this change, the integration, both practical and theoretical (in life and in outlook), of the individual into the group is completed. The age-old conflict between man and society has been resolved (Ollman, 107–08).

One problem in a solution along these lines is that the nature and possibilities of collective selfhood are drastically altered as the number of persons in the collectivity increases. In fact, organic civic virtue encounters the same problems as individualist and moral civic virtue, and its own besides.

1. Either conflicts of interest among individuals and groups in the collectivity do not exist, or else the collectivity must deal with

such conflicts. Among a large aggregate of persons the first looks to be impossible while the second would make organic civic virtue impossible.

2. As the number of persons in the aggregate increases, knowledge of the others and their concrete interests becomes increasingly difficult to come by. Even if Aymé's sisterhood were possible, presumably at some point the switchboard for sisterly communication would become jammed. And even if the communication channels could transmit all the messages between everyone composing the collective self, apprehending the overall good of that enormously complex collectivity would grow more and more difficult. In an association less fantastic than Aymé's sisterhood, that knowledge cannot be directly cognized; it requires theory.

3. In addition to these difficulties, which it shares with the other prescriptions, organic civic virtue has its own special difficulties of a psychological sort. Although knowledge of the absolute bounds of human consciousness is meager and views on this matter are highly controversial, the psychological processes for achieving collective self hood on a vast scale are so remote from human experience that without a convincing psychological and physiological model depicting the process in some detail, one is entitled to conclude that organic civic virtue belongs less in the domain of political science or political philosophy than, like Aymé's sisterhood, in the realm of fiction.

From Egoism to the General Good

We can now see why the obstacles to achieving civic virtue as a steady orientation among a large aggregate of persons have never been successfully overcome and are not likely to be. If one believes that governments among large aggregates of persons are necessary, desirable, and ought to be democratic, then one is compelled to search for alternative solutions. Moreover, since even with their much smaller citizen bodies city-states failed to overcome the obstacles to civic virtue in their actual political life (which contrasted

sharply with the civic ideals commended by their writers), it is difficult to resist the conclusion that to construct any regime on the assumption that civic virtue will steadily prevail would be folly.

One familiar alternative, which turns its back on the quest for
civic virtue, is to search for the general good through individual
egoism: Assume boldly that individuals care only for their own interests and cannot be made to seek the public good. While egoism
and conflicts of interest are lethal to civic virtue, might not it be possible, given certain structural arrangements, for an aggregate of
egoistic individualists all pursuing their own selfish advantage to
produce unwittingly an outcome in the best interests of all, and thus
in the public good? That this is possible was of course the famous
argument propounded in the original theory and program of European and American liberalism. Though most contemporary liberals
reject the argument in part or in whole, its influence has been profound, particularly because of the extraordinary impact of the normative theory of market capitalism developed by Adam Smith and
his neoclassical successors.

Perhaps the most enticing aspect of this solution is how it
seems to hurdle over the major obstacles to achieving civic virtue
among a large number of persons. If, given only the right social,
economic, and political structures, the general good will come
about as an unintended by-product of egoistic individuals, presumably the solution can work no matter how large the aggregate of persons involved.

Experience and analysis both reveal, however, that this astounding prescription for achieving the general good does not escape problems akin to those encountered in the older quest for civic
virtue. Problems arise because of a single troublesome condition
necessary to the success of the entire scheme: A "public" sphere of
collective decisions must still exist. Thus a condition of success is
the existence of a state and its government. Not being anarchists,
the classical and neoclassical liberals understood that at a minimum
the government of a state would be necessary to enact and enforce
laws and policies required for the existence of the fundamental reg-

ulative structures that are in turn necessary if the solution is to work.

For example, the government of the state must define and enforce the rights of ownership, maintain markets and competition, define and punish theft and certain other forms of wrongdoing (including conspiracies in restraint of trade), regulate the supply of currency, punish counterfeiting, and so on. Without the support of a state, the essential regulative structures of market capitalism would wither. As realists, classical liberals adopted this premise, as did their successors, and it is of critical importance. For it immediately poses a problem: what civic orientations are necessary in order for the government of the state to maintain the regulative structures that are necessary if individual egoism is to lead to the general welfare rather than to general ill-fare? Evidently, the appropriate civic orientations would need to have both an affective and a cognitive component. The affective component, sufficient to energize action, would be the thrust of self-interest. The cognitive component would be the belief that self-interest is best served by certain historically specific social and economic structures. In the normative theory of market capitalism these would include private ownership of economic resources and the competitive struggle of individuals and firms for maximum gain in an unregulated market for labor, land, commodities, and capital.

But at the level of concrete experience, the plausibility of the belief declines as the scale of the economy increases. Why should one believe that one's interests will be served best by striving with others in a market rather than by cooperating with others to rig the market by fixing prices? The chain of reasoning linking one's egoistic interests with those of other egoists acting in the market grows long and complex. To follow through that chain of reasoning requires logical and mathematical skills of a high order. The number of people who can appraise the technical validity of the neoclassical theory of general equilibrium is not, for all practical purposes, larger than those who can appraise the validity of Einstein's general theory of relativity. Is the theory plausible in the concrete situation—mine, yours, others? Evidently not. Adam Smith warned that if laws permit, businessmen will surely combine to bilk their customers. Why then should businessmen support laws that will prevent them from forming monopolies? Is it in their interest to do so? Should not farmers cooperate to gain higher incomes than a competitive market for their products would provide? Why should workers not combine to form trade unions, avoid competing in the market, and if possible push up the price of labor by collective action?

What is more, a system of competitive capitalism is unlikely to be sustained purely from the force of individual egoism. *To sustain the system itself requires benevolence, even altruism.* Why should the rational businessman, worker, or consumer obey the theory? Is it not perfectly rational, as I have just suggested, for a perfect egoist to seek monopoly, subsidies, exploitation, and other special privileges so long as they are to his own immediate benefit? The best that the theorist can say is that to permit these actions will not maximize the long-run benefit of the collectivity: society or consumers. But the practical force of the theoretical argument is weakened by the elaborate chain of reasoning it requires, and it is lethally flawed because even if the conclusion were true it would carry no weight with an egoist. If one's orientations are egoistic, why should one act in ways injurious to one's own interests simply because the results are harmful, in the long run, to the interests of others? By cultivating egoism, capitalism destroys the very orientations necessary to maintain the system itself.

Further, a capitalist order does not exist, and very likely cannot exist, without conscious cooperation on a small scale. But small-scale cooperation tends to generate orientations more favorable to norms of unselfishness. Organizations beget loyalties, attachments, sentiments of community and solidarity. The norms of individualistic egoism thus conflict with orientations more appropriate to community and solidarity, the notion of a common good, unselfishness, charity, pity, compassion. Because of this, the normative theory of capitalism labors under still another handicap: why should one support a system that violates the orientations one brings to relationships marked by intimacy, friendship, affection, love?

Now if the government of the state is democratic, then a majority of citizens, at least, would have to adhere to the proper beliefs. In practice, however, a democratic government would find it difficult to sustain the necessary structures unless the proper beliefs were widely diffused throughout most of the citizen body. For the larger the proportion of citizens who hold contrary beliefs and are willing to act on them—for example, to form labor unions, to organize monopolies, and to seek subsidies and other benefits from the government—the more difficult it becomes to maintain the necessary structures. As the number of opponents increases, then either disaffection and coercion also increase or the majority accommodates its policies to minority demands and the structures are allowed to diverge from the theoretical prescriptions that justify individual egoism and competitive capitalism as means for maximizing the general welfare. If the oppositional minority swells into a majority, then either the necessary structures will be altered or democracy must be abandoned so that the structure can be maintained by guardians independent of popular controls. In either case, the affiliation between democracy, liberty, and competitive capitalism would be severed and the historic program of liberalism would be rejected as a failure.

Two Unachieved Utopias

In order for the general welfare to be attained solely by means of individualist egoism strictly requires, according to the normative theories of market capitalism, certain regulative structures. These regulative structures exist in no democratic country, and probably exist in no country. Civic orientations sufficient to sustain them have either failed to develop or have never lasted long (Polanyi 1944). Instead, in all countries with privately owned, market-oriented economies the actual structures are a hodgepodge that cannot be shown by the normative theory of market capitalism to be either necessary or sufficient for achieving the general welfare. The verdict of public opinion reflected in civic orientations, regulative structures, and government policies in all democratic countries amounts to a decisive rejection of the Utopia of market capitalism.

At the same time, however, in no country, whether capitalist or socialist in its economic structures, has "socialist man" evolved with a "socialist consciousness" strong enough to sustain a steady commitment among workers to act for the collective benefit of "the working class," much less for "society" or "humanity." The most important advocate of the conception of an evolving working-class consciousness leading to the revolutionary transformation of capitalism, the inauguration of a socialist society, and the eventual liberation of mankind was, of course, Marx. As on many other questions, however, Marxist theoreticians radically disagree in their interpretation of precisely *how* proletarian consciousness is to develop. Thus in Lenin's view, the proletariat could not achieve a revolutionary socialist consciousness by its own efforts, and the task of inculcating the appropriate understanding in the working class must therefore be taken over by the political instrument of those who possessed an adequate theoretical understanding, ie., the party. At the other extreme, Rosa Luxemburg emphasized that revolutionary class consciousness would—and must be permitted to—develop more or less spontaneously. Gramsci, who developed a complex position somewhere between those of Lenin and Luxemburg, insisted that the proletariat must gain cultural "hegemony" over the bourgeoisie, a task for which it would require help from intellectuals and the party. Going even further than Lenin in some respects, Lukács assigned to the party the role not only of assisting the proletariat to acquire revolutionary consciousness but also of determining in behalf of the proletariat, whenever the working class was unable to do so itself, the correct consciousness required to complete its historical mission. While Gramsci's view to some extent foreshadowed the later evolution of the ideology and program of the Italian Communist party, the central function assigned to the party by Lenin and

Lukács is still defended by more orthodox Leninists. Thus Sánchez Vásquez flatly rejects the notion that the working class may gravitate spontaneously toward socialism and insists that the task of inculcating revolutionary class consciousness properly belongs to the party, whose members necessarily will often, like Marx and Engels, have their own class origins in the educated strata of the middle classes (1977, 239ff.).

Despite critical differences like these, probably all Marxists would agree that the civic orientations required in order to bring about socialism will be fostered by the concrete, everyday experiences of workers. The "objective" situation of the proletariat (clarified, to be sure, by Marxist theory) will enable workers to discover that their most fundamental interests are identical. Objectively speaking, workers form a single community on a vast, even a worldwide scale. Although theory may be required to clarify the objective nature of the workers' own interests, daily life helps them to develop an awareness of their objective interests. They become aware not only of their objective solidarity with one another but also of the inherent conflict between their own class interests and those of the owning class. Because the conflict of class interests is ineradicable under capitalism, the class awareness of workers will be transformed in time into a revolutionary class consciousness. Consciousness and action will reinforce one another, and in the fullness of time the working class will bring about socialism. Within the new socialist order, conflicting interests arising from class differences will cease to exist in an objective sense; finally, they will cease to exist subjectively as well (e.g., Sánchez Vásquez 1977, 134ff.; Balbus 1971, 167–70).

It is a lofty vision, made even nobler when viewed alongside the narrowly egoistic man assumed by the normative theory of market capitalism. Yet it is striking that in its assumptions about civic orientations, the one theory suffers from almost precisely the same defects as the other.

To begin with, a very high level of theoretical understanding would be required in order for workers to comprehend their interests in the way that Marxists describe. Many Marxists concede, in fact strongly insist on, the crucial role played by a "correct" theoretical understanding of the world. Without theory, how would a worker correctly apprehend his objective interests, his solidarity with other workers, the inherent conflict of interest with the bourgeoisie, and the solution of socialism? Yet just how workers are to acquire the theoretical understanding they need remains something of a mystery. Marx did not specify the process; the connection between the concrete experiences of workers and their ideas is hidden in one of the crucial black boxes of Marx's thought. Marxist theoreticians, as I suggested, are far from agreed on the contents of the black box. In fact, few try to specify its contents; they simply take the connection for granted.

However, the difficulty remains. Marx's theory is abstract and difficult—so much so that even scholars who devote their whole attention to it disagree on its meaning. Marxist theoreticians are notoriously contentious. Can one seriously believe that in order for socialism to be achieved, workers must become Marxist theoreticians—at the level, say, of Lenin, Gramsci, or Lukács? Few Marxists would make so preposterous an assumption. Yet if workers do not acquire a high level of theoretical understanding, how are they to appreciate the existence of objective class interests and the need for socialism?

Moreover, it is hard to escape the conclusion that if the proletariat is to fulfill the historical mission of the class assigned to it by Marx, many workers will have to act from purely altruistic intentions. Even with the aid of the theory, and all the more without it, the individual self-interest of each worker may not coincide with that of other workers, either under capitalism or under socialism. Even a worker who understands and accepts the theory might reasonably conclude that her individual interests, not merely in the short run but in the longer run of her own lifetime, are best served by raising wages and prices in her firm or industry at the expense of consumers, and thus other workers' real incomes. To say that a worker would not take such actions because they would harm other workers is to say that she would act altruistically.

The point is strengthened by the reluctance of Marx and later Marxists to specify boundaries for "the proletariat." Just as democratic philosophers have been prone to refer to "man" and "humanity," and thereby leave the demos completely unbounded, so Marxists refer to an unbounded proletariat, which is simply a global subset of man, humanity, "species man," and the like. Yet the more vast and unbounded the number of other workers who constitute "the working class," the less likely it is that any particular worker will really try to take their interests fully into account.

Finally, unless workers are expected to act from altruistic intentions, why should a particular worker join in the revolutionary effort, the class actions, if without doing so he can gain the benefits resulting from the actions of other workers? (Olson 1965).

Given the first two difficulties, it is not surprising that although a full century has passed since Marx wrote, in no democratic country have workers come to form a perfectly cohesive bloc. As we saw in chapter 4, no matter how it may be defined, the working class is generally crosscut by a variety of other cleavages, such as religion, region, language, ethnic group, ideology, and so on. The theoretical solidarity of the working class that Marx believed necessary for socialism is profoundly weakened by these other attachments and "subjective" interests. Among other things, the solidarity of workers as a class is undercut by their attachments to smaller groups whose interests, in their view, do not necessarily coincide with those of the "working class as a whole." The effort to transfer the loyalty and solidarity of the smaller groups to the larger aggregate constituted by the "working class" is often defeated by the very existence of strong loyalties within the smaller group itself. Over against the hypothetical interests of the great amorphous aggregate of workers are the concrete attachments to smaller aggregates like neighborhood, workplace, craft, labor union, or church; and even when solidarity expands to a more inclusive aggregate more often than not the larger group is still no more than a fragment of the working class as a whole.

Consequently, just as the enthusiasm for democracy of some nineteenth-century liberal economists was dampened by the anticipation—which proved to be correct—that if workers were granted the franchise they would try to compel governments to violate the normative requirements of liberal economic theory, so Marxists have sometimes rejected the institutions of democracy on essentially the same grounds. In their view, if workers cannot be expected to acquire spontaneously a correct grasp of theory, the task of instruction will have to be performed by others. What is needed is a kind of "collective intellectual," that is, the party. (Sánchez Vásquez, 254) However, what begins as justification for a party sometimes ends as a rationalization for a hegemonic party in a regime where all the underlying tendencies toward organizational pluralism in politics, economic life, and society in general are repressed because they are manifestations of either the correctly perceived but historically retrograde interests of the bourgeoisie or the false consciousness of the proletariat. Just as the attempt to apply the normative theory of market capitalism at all costs would require its advocates to sever the liberal connection between democracy, liberty, and capitalism, so the attempt to ensure at all costs that the working class act according to a "correct" revolutionary consciousness cuts the connection Marx explicitly made between democracy and socialism.

Consensus on Regulative Structures and Principles

The upshot of the argument so far is this. No solution to the problem of attaining the general good in a democratic country can be judged satisfactory if it requires civic orientations of a kind that could reasonably be expected to exist only if citizens (1) must live exclusively in small and completely autonomous polities, each a community of tightly bonded individuals; (2) must have no conflicts of interest, either objective or subjective; (3) must be either steadily altruistic or completely egoistic in their public affairs; or (4) must be highly proficient social theorists or philosophers. Let me refer to a solution that makes one or more of these demands as a prescription of Type I. A weak prescription of Type I might meet only one criterion; a strong prescription would meet all four. All the proposals examined so far are moderately strong prescriptions of Type I and are therefore unsatisfactory.

Now imagine a Type II that violates all four criteria. Type II might be called a prescription for a large-scale system if it were consistent with these assumptions:

1. Among the units that make up a satisfactory political system in the foreseeable future, some must be at least as large as a country, and some must be even larger.

2. In democratic countries, political conflicts are certain to exist.

3. Most citizens will not be either steadily altruistic or completely egoistic in public affairs.

And 4. Most citizens are unlikely to be highly competent social theorists or political philosophers.

The upshot of the previous argument is that only a Type II prescription for democratic pluralism can be satisfactory. Yet not all Type II prescriptions need be satisfactory. In a moment I shall propose a fifth criterion for a minimally satisfactory Type II prescription. But first let me say a word about each of the four assumptions.

1. Reasons for making the first assumption were set out in chapter 2. It is no doubt the least controversial of the lot. Yet though not very controversial, it is among the fundamental causes of the problem of democratic pluralism. It is also a reason, as we have just seen, why a prescription containing any of the other possible elements in a Type I theory is unsatisfactory.

2. In considering the second assumption, we need to distinguish between political conflicts over particular issues and conflicts over the regulative structures and principles of a society. Conflict over the first may lead to conflict over the second, as with slavery and the American Civil War, but it need not. For even though a

democratic country cannot possibly eliminate political conflicts over particular issues, a country's fundamental regulative principles and structures might receive such widespread support as to survive particular controversies. In some countries, such as the United States and the Scandinavian countries, a moderately high level of support for certain regulative principles and structures has been sustained over fairly long periods, although that consensus may now be breaking down, particularly in the United States. Consequently, we should not rule out the possibility that in countries where polyarchy has existed and the ideology of democracy has been dominant for several generations or more, consensus may develop on new regulative structures and principles that reflect a greater awareness of the interdependence of individual and common interests.

It goes without saying that a regulative consensus is not immutable. Exogenous factors may alter principles or structures. Changes in the one introduce strains that weaken the other. A period of decaying consensus may, however, be followed by a long period of stability in the consensus on regulative principles and structures. Major transitions of this kind in American history would include the Revolution, the Constitutional Convention, the Civil War, the election of 1896, and the New Deal.

3. Consensus on regulative structures and principles is entirely consistent with the third assumption. In fact, none of the fundamental types of civic orientations described earlier need steadily prevail. Political life may actually benefit from a mix of orientations that encourage citizens to be concerned for both their own particular interests and the broader good of the collectivity. Not only might different citizens be steadily animated by different orientations, but different roles, events, situations, processes, and structures might evoke different orientations in the same citizen. Thus citizens strongly animated in particular conflicts by individual or group egoism might, in considering regulative structures and principles, give more weight to "moral" judgments about what would be best for the collectivity.

As an example, while a good deal of the behavior of Americans in political conflicts over particular issues can be explained as a result of individual and group egoism, in national elections, as Kinder and Kiewiet have shown, citizens often seem to be animated by a concern for what is best for the country, independent of the specific consequences for themselves and their families (Kinder and Kiewiet 1981; see also Schlozman and Verba 1979, 352ff.). If many American citizens behave "sociotropically" rather than egoistically in national elections, it is plausible to think that their support for regulative structures and principles might be strongly animated by considerations, however vague, of what would be best for the country as a whole.

4. Although regulative principles may resemble abstract theorems of the kind found in philosophical or theoretical argument, the two ought not to be confused. Political philosophers often write as if their abstract principles can be made to prevail in the world from the persuasiveness of their own reasoning. However, the effects of formal political theorizing on civic orientations and regulative principles are rather obscure, and there is scant reason for thinking that philosophical theories have much immediate consequence for either. Sometimes the influence may run the other way, and late in the game; as Hegel remarked, the owl of Minerva flies at dusk. However that may be, in speaking of a consensus on regulative structures and principles we must not imagine a people convinced of their political beliefs by reasoning abstractly from premises to formal principles, but rather a system of beliefs widely diffused among a people whose commitments may vary in strength and clarity and yet who interpret the world, in a loose way, through the lens of their beliefs. A people guided in public life by their commitments to certain general principles and structures can cope daily with ambiguities and inconsistencies that a philosopher would make into a career. A political consensus is not a philosophical treatise but part of a political culture into which most people, not least those highly influential in shaping opinions and decisions, are more or less adequately socialized. Consequently, to require a consensus on regulative principles and structures does not mean that citizens must

be competent theorists or philosophers, and it therefore need not violate the fourth assumption for a prescription of Type II.

Yet a solution consistent only with these four requirements could easily be unsatisfactory on other grounds. To be minimally satisfactory, a prescription of Type II would have to be appraised according to at least one more requirement.

5. Regulative structures and principles are less satisfactory to the extent that they preserve or create among citizens long-run conflicts in their fundamental interests, either objectively or subjectively; conversely, the more that regulative structures and principles reduce such conflicts of interest, both objectively and subjectively, the better they are.

Although the fifth requirement on first glance might appear to bring in the second requirement of Type I prescriptions by the back door, it is consistent with the second and weaker assumption of Type II prescriptions.

Because the language of (5) is loose, to apply it demands difficult and controversial judgments. Only extreme cases are easy to judge. For example, most people would surely agree that the regulative structures of American slavery created a long-run conflict of fundamental interests between slaveholders and slaves, no matter how nicely some masters sometimes treated some slaves. To reduce that fundamental conflict of interests, slavery necessarily had to be abolished. The regulative institutions of White supremacy that followed created a new form of objective conflict in fundamental interests—a valid judgment even if some Blacks and many Whites believed that White supremacy was in the interests of both races. Like slavery, the regulative institutions of White supremacy had to be abolished in order to reduce the fundamental conflict of interests between blacks and whites. Unlike slavery and White supremacy, however, in many cases the judgments required in order to apply the criterion will be much more complex and far more contestable.

Difficult as the fifth criterion is to interpret and to apply, something like it is essential. For the criterion compels us to inquire whether conflicts over the general good stem primarily from faulty perceptions and might therefore be diminished by better understanding or instead are fundamental conflicts of interest built into the regulative structures and principles themselves and can therefore be reduced, if at all, only by structural changes or new regulative principles or both. The fundamental conflict of interest in the prisoners' dilemma would not be reduced, at least among rational prisoners, by exhorting them to be nicer to one another. The conflict is built into the very structure of a situation that prevents them from cooperating to achieve their common good. Based on a faulty diagnosis, a prescription for changing attitudes without changing structures is a prescription for "false consciousness."

As we have seen, prescriptions for achieving the public good vary in how much importance they attach to changing civic orientations rather than altering regulative structures. Prescriptions for changing civic orientations also vary from some that seem to propose little beyond philosophical guidance to others promising that the desired changes in civic orientation will automatically result from changing certain regulative structures. In a very rough way, differences like these tend to distinguish liberal and radical proposals for achieving the public good. Liberals, like conservatives, tend to believe that in many democratic countries with capitalist economies the general good could be attained if only more people correctly understood that their long-run interests are not fundamentally conflicting but basically complementary. In this view, what is needed is a big change in civic consciousness but only small changes in the basic regulative principles and structures. On the other hand, many socialists and by definition all Marxists tend to believe that the long-run interests of the working class necessarily conflict fundamentally with the interests of those who own and operate privately owned business firms. In this view only a transformation of the regulative structures can eliminate this conflict of fundamental interests between workers and owners; and workers who accept liberal or conservative prescriptions for achieving the public good simply exhibit a false consciousness that is not correctly based in objective conditions.

Any proposal for achieving the general good in a democratic country must be judged unsatisfactory if no general good exists because the regulative structures create long-run conflicts of fundamental interests among citizens. In this circumstance, the more rational citizens are, the more that exhorting them to strive for the general good is a useless remedy; and the more that such exhortation succeeds in changing civic orientations and bringing about a consensus on regulative principles and structures, the more deceptive the exhortation and the more meretricious the consensus.

8

Remedies

In a political system as large as a country, a plurality of relatively independent organizations is necessary not only for mutual control but also for the democratic process. Applied on the scale of a country, the democratic process in turn makes relatively independent organizations both possible and inevitable. Yet a problem arises—which I have called the problem of democratic pluralism—because while necessary, desirable, and inevitable in a democratic order, organizational pluralism may also play a part in stabilizing inequalities, deforming civic consciousness, distorting the public agenda, and alienating final control over the public agenda by the citizen body.

For reasons explored in chapter 3, the specific shape of the problem varies in different democratic countries. Because of variations in patterns of conflict and cleavage, concrete political institutions, and the inclusiveness and concentration of organizations, remedies that may be appropriate in one country may be unnecessary or undesirable in another. In this final chapter, therefore, I want to focus on possible remedies appropriate to the shape of the problem of democratic pluralism in the United States.

Limiting Factors

Certain remedies that many people find attractive must be ruled out because of limiting factors. By a limiting factor I mean something that is either inherent in democratic pluralism or necessary to its existence, so that in order to remove it we should have to destroy democratic pluralism itself. One such limiting factor is of course democracy or, more accurately, the attempt to apply the democratic process to the government of a country. To deal with the problem of democratic pluralism by getting rid of large-scale democracy, as some small-scale democrats seem to envision, would eliminate the problem but not solve it. We would then face a far more formidable difficulty. If in order to remedy the defects of organizational pluralism as it now exists in the United States we were simply to abandon the effort to create large-scale democracy, we would have to adopt one of three alternatives: abolish the state altogether; create a nondemocratic state; or break the United States into somewhere between a thousand and a hundred thousand completely autonomous microstates. Since each of these alternatives would leave most Americans much worse off and would surely re-create, though in different form, all the defects now attributed to organizational pluralism, I accept as an irremovable limit on solutions the continuation of the American experiment with large-scale democracy.

Following from the first limit is a second, or rather a set of limits: the democratic dilemmas described in chapter 5. When different groups of citizens set forth conflicting claims to autonomy and control, principles drawn from democratic ideas, general theories of justice, or specific constitutional principles will not necessarily yield a solution that is either unambiguous or incontestably desirable. For example, we cannot properly deny political autonomy and control to certain citizens on the purely substantive ground that they are able thereby to inflict harm on others; for it is likely that any alternative allocation of autonomy and control will also enable some people to harm others. To propose that we resolve such issues on purely utilitarian grounds raises both substantive and procedural problems. Substantively, aside from all the familiar difficulties in a utilitarian appraisal of costs and benefits a more basic difficulty arises when a strictly utilitarian solution confronts claims based on fundamental rights. In addition, some sort of procedure is needed for arriving at judgments about such cases. Even if the legitimacy of the majority principle were granted, to propose that all jurisdictional issues be settled by a majority decision runs squarely into the question, Which majority is rightfully entitled to settle jurisdictional questions? If one set of contestants is more numerous and more inclusive than another, should the more inclusive majority always prevail? To justify control by the more inclusive majority as invariably a matter of right is easily rebutted by counterexamples. And a justification based only on utilitarian considerations, such as "the greatest good of the greatest number," will once again clash with claims to autonomy justified by appeals to fundamental rights.

In the same way, to justify a grant of political autonomy on the utilitarian ground that concentration of power and political resources is dangerous, and decentralization is therefore desirable, fails to meet the argument that on some matters, including fundamental rights, uniformity *is* desirable; and uniformity requires centralization and concentration. And so on. I do not mean to imply that reasonable solutions can never be found. Moreover, certain constitutional and political principles would help to guide a country through its conflicts over autonomy and control. But we cannot expect any solution to the problem of democratic pluralism to escape scot-free from the fundamental democratic dilemmas described in chapter 5. For we live in a world where ideal solutions frequently cannot be found, even at the theoretical level. We may, nonetheless, sometimes arrive at satisfactory solutions.

Closely associated with the first two limits is a third. For reasons discussed in the last chapter, we must reject Type I solutions altogether. Yet not all Type II solutions for large-scale democracies are equally desirable.

Finally, and partly as a consequence of the others, a limit is set by the need for some decentralization of economic decisions to relatively autonomous units, including productive enterprises, and consequently also for a system of market controls. The need for decentralization and markets limits solutions not only for economies in which economic enterprises are mainly owned privately but also for those in which the means of production are mainly owned socially or publicly. For reasons explored in chapter 6, a centrally directed economy, whether owned privately or publicly, is likely to be incompatible in the long run with the existence of democratic controls. For either the Guardians at the Center must be made independent of democratic controls in order to insure that they can "rationally" direct all important economic decisions from the Center, in which case the incompatibility exists by definition; or else they *are* subject to democratic controls, in which case (as I argued in chapter 6) popular and legislative pressures would make a mishmash of the detailed, "rational," comprehensive plans of the Guardians. If on these (and other) grounds we reject the solution of a centrally directed economy, it follows that decentralization of important economic decisions is necessary.

Decentralization means, of course, that decision makers at some centers other than *the* Center exercise some autonomy over some decisions. Like the Center in a command economy, these relatively autonomous centers might constitute *the* Center of a local command economy. However, this solution would not only recreate, though on a smaller scale, the problem of how the control of the Guardians in a centrally directed economy can be reconciled with democratic controls; it would also generate a new problem: coordination. Either the decisions of the various centers would not require coordination; or the centers would (somehow) spontaneously coordinate their decisions without benefit of any external controls; or their decisions would be coordinated by some system of external controls that would limit, in some respects, the autonomy of the decision makers at the various centers.

As solutions in a complex economy, the first two are absurd, and so far as I am aware, no satisfactory model exists along either line. External controls might be exercised by higher governmental officials, by market forces, or by both. If market controls were entirely absent, an impossible burden of information and communication would be placed on higher officials responsible for coordinating the decisions of officials in the relatively autonomous centers. Moreover, in order to enforce their coordinating decisions, higher officials would need effective sanctions, and these would necessarily reduce the autonomy of the various centers. Without some system of market controls, then, not only would a decentralized economy be highly inefficient but, in order to achieve more efficient coordination, one of two developments would almost certainly occur in the long run. Either the relatively decentralized system would be transformed into something much closer to a centrally directed economy; or else some of the heavy burden of coordination would be shifted from higher officials of government onto the market. If for reasons already considered we reject the one alternative, only the other remains, and our fourth limit follows.

If we accept these limits, would it be possible to remedy the defects of organizational pluralism in the United States?

Inequalities in Political Resources

The Standard Solution: Floors and Ceilings

If the problem of inequality in political resources is old and familiar, so also are many of the remedies. The classical remedy was to ensure that at least one crucial political resource, the vote, would be equally distributed among all citizens. While universal and equal suffrage is necessary for the democratic process, however, it has long been known to be insufficient because the vote is only one kind of political resource. Because social resources are unequally distributed, and because many kinds of social resources can be converted into political resources, political resources other than the vote are unequally distributed.

A more recent remedy is to impose minima and maxima on political resources. By putting floors under the social resources available to all citizens—for example, by universal, free, compulsory education and a basic income supplied by social security and welfare payments—minimal political resources are guaranteed to all citizens. In addition, ceilings are placed on the extent to which certain social resources, mainly money, can legally be converted into political resources—for example, by limits on campaign contributions.

Only with the suffrage, however, have the floor and the ceiling been brought together. With other resources, the difference between minima and maxima allows great inequalities in social resources to be converted into great inequalities in political resources. For example, differences in education, occupation, financial resources, and access to organizations greatly affect the extent to which different American citizens participate in political life, the ways in which they participate, and their effectiveness in gaining a response from government officials. Education appears to have the greatest impact on political participation (Wolfinger and Rosenstone 1980, 23ff.); and education is loosely correlated with other resources: occupation, income, and access to organizations. Since it would be preposterous to reduce inequalities in political resources by imposing a ceiling on education, the alternative is substantially to increase the minimum level of education, which would require a far larger allocation of resources than at present to the task of re-educating the less educated.

Or consider financial resources. Beyond a moderate level income does not seem to have much effect on *levels* of participation. But access to money enables some people to participate more effectively in certain ways—by campaign contributions, for example. To be sure, the effects of large campaign contributions are often exaggerated. In spite of prevailing myths, a candidate does not often become the lackey of a large donor; what a contributor often does gain, however, is the potential influence provided by easier access to an elected official and a more sympathetic consideraton of the donor's requests (Staebler 1979, 22). And although the legal ceilings on campaign contributions are now far below the financial resources of the rich, they are well above the financial resources of most citizens. To bring the ceilings down to the level suitable to citizens of median income would still leave the limits much above the level of the most disadvantaged, and in addition might drastically reduce campaigning. Inequalities in financial and organizational resources also generate inequalities in opportunities to influence the beliefs and actions of other citizens. Finally, differences in financial resources contribute to differences in education, for wealthier citizens and communities can afford to spend more on the education of their children, and do so. As a result, differences in influence are somewhat self-maintaining.

The Extent of Economic Inequality among Americans
That gross economic inequality has persisted among Americans for many generations is hardly an obscure or even highly contestable fact. In the 1890s the Farmers' Alliance and the Populists publicized data showing great inequality in the distribution of wealth and income. Scholars also published estimates; in 1893 one political economist calculated that 0.33 percent of the population owned 20 percent of the national wealth, while 52 percent owned only 5 percent (Pollack 1962, 76). Since that time, and particularly during the last twenty years or so, the data have become more reliable, more easily accessible, and probably better known. Familiar as they may be, the figures bear repeating.

Despite widespread views to the contrary, the net effect of taxes and transfer payments in altering the distribution of wealth and income has been comparatively modest. This is not to say that transfer payments are of trivial importance, for they are not. As in many European countries, in the United States taxes and transfer payments have become important instruments of public policy. As a proportion of total personal income, transfer payments nearly doubled between 1965 and 1977, increasing from 7.6 percent in 1965 to 13.8 percent in 1977. Most of this increase was in retirement benefits, which constituted 6.4 percent of personal income in 1965 and 11.3 percent in 1977. However, transfers of other kinds—primarily unemployment compensation and income maintenance programs, including food stamps—also increased (U.S. Census Bureau 1980, 446). The main effect of transfer payments on incomes, then, has been to sustain the incomes of the elderly and the bottom fifth of households (Thurow 1980, 157–60).

After half a century of the American welfare state, however, the after-tax distribution of wealth and income remains highly unequal.

Because the largest share of transfer payments draws on payroll taxes, which are progressive only in the lower range of wage and salary income and regressive beyond that range, the main effect is to redistribute income within the bottom half, principally from employed workers to retired and disabled persons. The bottom one-fifth of households, which received 4.1 percent of per capita household income in 1948, still received only 5.6 percent nearly three decades later in 1977 (Thurow, ibid.). These figures do not include income from accrued capital gains, which more than double the income share of the top 1 percent of all households (Pechman and Okner 1974, 46; Thurow, 168). Of course capital gains reflect wealth. Though wealth is even more unequally distributed than income, like income the distribution of wealth has not undergone much change. The top 1 percent of Americans owned 23.3 percent of personal wealth in 1945 and 20.7 percent in 1972. About 4 percent of the adult population own more than a third of all financial assets. The top 1 percent own 57 percent of all corporate stock, 60 percent of all bonds, and 26 percent of all net worth (U.S. Census Bureau 1980, 470). It is sometimes contended that figures like these exaggerate inequality because people acquire wealth as they grow older, and inequality in wealth is therefore mainly a function of age. The fact is, however, the wealth is distributed just as unequally within age groups as for the adult population as a whole (Smith et al. 1973, 7).

Sometimes findings like these are thought to demonstrate the existence of a ruling class. They do not. What they demonstrate is the existence of great inequality in the distribution of economic resources; and insofar as economic resources are convertible to political resources, the figures also demonstrate severe inequality in the distribution of political resources. There is no satisfactory formula for specifying an average rate at which economic resources can be converted into political resources. Probably none can be constructed. But consider the following. In 1969, the latest year for which good data seem to be available, the average net worth of all adults, or 122 million persons, was $25,000. For 95.6 percent of all adults, comprising 117 million persons, it was $17,000. At the same time, 103,000 persons comprising the wealthiest 0.1 percent of the adult population had a mean net worth of around $2,446,000 (calculated from Smith et al., table 1). Thus the average person in the wealthiest stratum had almost 100 times the economic resources of the average American citizen, and 144 times the economic resources of most citizens. Even if the conversion rate from economic to political resources were low and decreasing, such a distribution would create distinctly unequal classes of citizens.

In the election system that prevailed in Prussia from 1850 to 1918, voters were divided into three strata based on property, each of which was entitled to one-third of the popularly elected representatives. The smallest and wealthiest stratum comprised around 5 percent of the voters, the intermediate stratum around 13 percent, and the largest and poorest around 82 percent. Thus 18 percent of the voters were guaranteed 67 percent of the representatives. Not surprisingly, this system engendered deep resentments that helped to poison political life both in Prussia and in the Reich (Sternberger and Vogel 1969, table A-4, p. 348; Rokkan 1962, 76–77). If such a system were proposed for the United States, Americans would be outraged and their outrage would be fully justified on democratic grounds; for institutionalizing voting inequality in this way violates the most elementary requirements for political equality in a democratic republic. But does not the institutionalization of inequalities in wealth and income, and thus in political resources, also violate these requirements?

How Economic Inequality Has Been Reduced in Some Democratic Countries
In some democratic countries, the distribution of income, one of the prime components in economic inequality, is markedly less unequal than in the United States. These countries include the Netherlands, Sweden, Norway, Britain, and Japan. It follows that the extent of economic inequality in the United States is not inherent either in a market-oriented and privately owned economy or in polyarchy and organizational pluralism.

The explanation for the difference, as David Cameron has shown, is primarily political. Among the twelve democratic countries he examined, the distribution of after-tax income is only weakly related to the level of economic production. To be sure, countries like Italy and Spain have lower levels of per capita gross domestic product and greater inequality in incomes. But among all twelve countries the relation is so slight as to offer little hope that income inequality can be significantly reduced by economic growth. Moreover, despite plausible hypotheses to the contrary, income inequality is not related (either positively or negatively) to high rates of growth; or (positively) to the proportion of young people receiving higher education; or (negatively) to the extent of middle-class advantage in access to higher education. *The most important factor by far is simply the extent to which social democratic and labor parties have played a significant role in the government*: income inequality tends to be least in countries where they have. By means of higher levels of employment and expenditures on social security, health, and income maintenance, governments responsive to social democratic and labor parties have raised the after-tax incomes of the bottom fifth; and by higher marginal tax rates on incomes they have reduced the after-tax incomes of the top fifth (Cameron 1980).

For all the emphasis on equality in the American public ideology, the United States lags well behind a number of other democratic countries in reducing economic inequality. It is a striking fact that the presence of vast disparities in wealth and income, and so in political resources, has never become a highly salient issue in American politics or, certainly, a persistent one. When concern has surfaced in mainstream politics it has not led to much more than rhetorical denunciation: the only lasting product of Theodore Roosevelt's renowned attack on "malefactors of great wealth" was the phrase itself.

Why Economic Inequality Is Not a Political Issue among Americans
To explain why economic inequality has not been an issue in American politics, one must go beyond the standard response of the Left

that Americans have been brainwashed (or coerced) by the wealthy, an explanation that is sometimes also used to account for the inability of a socialist movement to make headway in the United States. The weakness of this response, as I pointed out in chapter 3, is that it fails to explain why in practically every European country privileged elites who stood at the top of a concentration of wealth, income, status, education, and authority in government that was generally far more acute than in the United States nevertheless were unable to prevent politically important socialist movements from developing; or why socialist movements in many of these countries succeeded in making a political issue of distributive questions; or why in some European countries socialist movements brought about considerably more redistribution than reform movements have ever managed to achieve in the United States. If the United States is a deviant case, its deviance cannot logically be attributed to a historical factor common to both the United States and European countries.

The United States did deviate from European countries, however, in at least one crucial respect: its ideological development. It is probably in this singularity that we must search for an explanation. From the American Revolution onward, the ancient problem posed by the presence of unequal wealth in a republic was met by at least three different ideological perspectives. In the ideology of Federalist republicanism, social and economic stratification was an inevitable, natural, and (within limits) desirable fact of social life to which politics, even in a republic, must adapt. So John Adams. At the other extreme, an occasional radical democrat like Thomas Skidmore contended that inequalities in the distribution of property were a definite threat to republican government, that property rights were subordinate to the fundamental right of self-government, and that in order to prevent gross inequality and preserve a republican polity, the government should intervene in a systematic way to regulate the distribution of property.

Aspects of both these perspectives were fused in the ideology of agrarian democratic republicanism that developed under the tutelage of men like Jefferson, Madison, and the writer John Taylor, Jefferson's ally. These advocates of an agrarian democratic republic agreed that social and economic inequalities would, if allowed to go unchecked, undermine the political equality they assumed to be essential to a democratic republic. In their view, however, the best guarantee of republican government was a body of citizens whose freedom and independence rested on individual ownership of property in land: a body of free farmers. The agrarian democratic republicans were not wildly unrealistic in believing that such a body of citizens could and would exist in the United States—among white males, at any rate. But in direct opposition to radical democrats like Skidmore, their solution did not seem to them to require direct government regulation of wealth or incomes. For the most important element in their solution lay readily at hand; it fit neatly into Locke's justification for property, and therefore (unlike Skidmore) it required no challenge to the primacy of property rights.

This providential element, which existed independent of human intentions, was the seemingly limitless supply of comparatively cheap land. As in Locke's justification of private property, but quite unlike the actual situation in Locke's England (or in any European country), in America the availability of land depended much less on conscious civic deliberation and design than on the bounty of nature. To be sure, the government might have to intervene to ensure that citizens would have adequate opportunities to acquire property in land. Opening up and protecting access to the land by (white) settlers would of course require some action by the federal government. But in contrast to Skidmore's vision of a democratic government that would deliberately regulate the distribution of wealth in order to insure political equality, in the ideology of agrarian democratic republicanism political equality would be an inevitable by-product of an equal opportunity to acquire property.

Now a key assumption of this solution was an implied boundary that sharply distinguished political from economic life, public matters from private affairs, and a sector of social relations in which authority definitely ought to be democratic from a sector in which it need not be. The polity, which had to do with public affairs, ought of course to be governed democratically by its citizens. The economy, however, constituted a sphere of private relationships in which productive enterprises (that is, farms) ought to be governed by their owners; and owners were entitled to govern not only themselves but any other adults who might choose freely to associate themselves in the enterprise. Naturally if the economic order had been seen as public, not private, the entire assumption would have broken down. But in the agrarian society the distinction between the public and political on the one side and the private economy of farming was hardly a contestable matter.

While Skidmore's solution of regulating distribution won almost no support, the solution of equal opportunity to acquire a farm and, as a result, to become the political equal, in a rough sense, of other farming citizens quickly gained a wide following. A fundamental and lasting way of thinking about solutions to the dynamics of inequality entered deeply into American national consciousness (cf. Pole 1978, 117–47). To be sure, the realities of American life diverged, sometimes quite visibly, from what Richard Hofstadter called "the agrarian myth" (1955, 23ff.). Most notably, a civic equality derived from an equal opportunity to acquire property in land offered no solution to the inequalities that prevailed both in the cities and in the slave economy of the South. If either the economy of urban commerce and finance or the economy of slavery were to spread, the social foundations of an agrarian democratic republic would be destroyed. In the face of dangers like these, some who endorsed the emerging ideology recognized that policies might be needed to check the accumulation of wealth among the few at the expense of general equality among the many. Thus Noah Webster contended that "an equality of property, with a necessity of alienation, constantly operating to destroy combinations of powerful families, is the very soul of a republic" (Stourzh 1970 in Pocock 1975, 534). And, as Hamilton's program came clearly into view, an alarmed Madison proposed that laws be enacted to withhold "unnecessary opportunities for the few to increase the inequality of property by

an immoderate, and especially unmerited, accumulation of riches."
Laws should silently "reduce extreme wealth towards a state of mediocrity, and raise indigence towards a state of comfort" (Pole, 122).
In effect, Madison proposed that there should be both a floor and
ceiling on wealth.

Yet nothing much ever came of these ideas. To explain why proposals for directly regulating the distribution of wealth came to
nothing, we need to look beyond the fact that some of the best-
known advocates of the ideology of agrarian democratic republicanism were often landholders of substance and sometimes slave-
owners as well. For the socioeconomic position of the advocates fails
to account for the broad acceptance of their views and the rejection
of solutions like Skidmore's. In understanding why the agrarian
myth and its solution of equal opportunity won out over its rivals, it
is important to keep in mind that even by 1820, 92 percent of the
American people still lived in rural areas and over 70 percent of the
work force was engaged in farming; in fact, people in farming occupations remained a majority of the work force until the 1870s.

To farmers, the ideology would have made a great deal of
sense. To begin with, equal access to land was obviously a far easier
policy for state and federal governments to carry out than attempting to set limits on landholdings. The idea of equal opportunity to
acquire land was also consistent with the right to property; in contrast, as Skidmore himself made clear, to regulate distribution by
limiting ownership challenged the sanctity of that right. In addition,
equal opportunity appealed to the strength of acquisitive desires
and to the social value of stimulating incentives for hard work, risk
taking, foresight, and efficiency; whereas the main appeal of regulating distribution would be either envy or the abstract moral ideal of
political equality.

Equal opportunity would also have fit better with a farmer's
sense that successful farming ought to be rewarded, while putting
floors and ceilings on wealth would have looked like rewarding
failure and penalizing success. Moreover, if there were a large supply of cheap land accessible to those willing to make the effort to

acquire, develop, and work it, in a society of free farmers the size of farms would be to some extent self-limiting anyway. Finally, while the policies of federal, state, and local governments were not unimportant to farmers, farmers were remarkably independent of all governments, which by European standards had almost no coercive means they could successfully apply against any significant group of recalcitrant white citizens, particularly farmers. Taken all around, then, it must have seemed reasonable for citizens associated with farming—and most citizens were—to believe that if the government were to do no more than provide an equal opportunity for citizens to acquire land, they would all have a rough equality—at least would not be dangerously unequal—in their access to political resources.

This perspective became so deeply rooted that by the 1890s when the social foundations of agrarian republicanism were visibly disappearing, neither the Greenback movement, the Farmers' Alliance, nor the Populists endorsed the idea of deliberately redistributing wealth and income, even though they turned, far more than their predecessors had ever done, directly to the government for assistance. It is true that among the items in the platform of the Alliance and the Populists was a call for a "graduated income tax." But the income tax was so minor an objective that the historians of the agrarian revolt have virtually ignored it (Hicks 1961, Goodwyn 1976, Pollack). The main thrust of the agrarian movement was not to put a ceiling on the accumulation of private wealth but to construct a low floor under farmers' incomes.

Even so, the Populist challenge was decisively defeated. Farmers shrank into an even smaller fraction of the population (3.3 percent of all households in 1978). Farming was more and more transformed into a business that became fully integrated into the new economic order of commercial, industrial, and financial capitalism. Ironically, however, with astonishing ease the older ideology was adapted to the radically different structure of the new economic order. As before, political equality would prevail among a citizen body of property owners. As before, the task of government was to ensure fair opportunities to acquire property—in consumer goods, homes, business enterprises, securities, and so on. As before, radical democrats and socialists who proposed that wealth be more directly regulated in order to ensure political equality among citizens were, like Skidmore a century earlier, a minority voice outside the mainstream of American political life.

Yet if discrepancies had already existed between ideology and reality during the agrarian period, by 1900 economic inequality had become immense, and it has remained so to the present day.

Why Economic Inequality May Become a Political Issue
Despite the fact that the unequal distribution of economic resources, and hence political resources, has never become a steady and major issue in American political life, there are reasons for thinking that it may become so in the future. To begin with, because the facts will not go away it would take only a slight shift in public concern to bring them to the forefront of political discussion and public attention, in the same way that rates of inflation, changes in the consumer price index, unemployment figures, budget deficits, and so on have been given currency. If economic growth were persistently low, distributive issues would probably become more urgent; for when everyone's slice of pie is smaller than expected, more people will be inclined to wonder whether their own slice has been fairly apportioned.

In addition, certain changes in the way the economy is likely to be perceived in the future would almost certainly help to make distributive issues more salient. In the ideology adapted from agrarian democratic republicanism the economy is perceived to be a "private" sector sharply distinct from the public sector of government and politics. But a distinction that no doubt seemed intuitively correct in the agrarian order now clashes much more forcefully with the actualities of economic relations in the economic order of corporate capitalism. While the distinction between public and private relations not only retains its usefulness but becomes even more crucial than before, it is surely a misperception to see large economic structures as private, for, like the government of the state, in a realistic sense they are public.

Consider economic growth. In his monumental statistical study of the sources of economic growth in the United States from 1929– 1969, Denison found that total national income grew at an annual rate of 3.33%. A little more than half of the annual increase Denison accounted for by changes in inputs of labor and capital. Of these inputs, changes in labor inputs were considerably more important than changes in capital inputs: 1.3% as against 0.5% for capital inputs. Of the labor inputs, changes in the amount of labor employed added about one percent annually to national income. The increased educational levels of the employed added another 0.4%. Together, these were more than sufficient to offset small losses resulting from a shortening of the hours of work during this period. A little less than half the annual increase in national income—1.5% to be exact—Denison accounted for by increases in output per unit of input, or what most of us would call greater productivity or increased efficiency. Of the factors that produced greater productivity, the largest (accounting for an annual increase in national income of 0.9 percent) is attributed to advances in knowledge (plus factors not elsewhere classified). Economies of scale accounted for slightly under 0.4 percent (calculated from Denison 1974, table 9-4, p. 127).

It is immediately obvious that little growth in the American economy can be attributed to the actions of particular individuals. Certainly growth is not attributable primarily to the insight, foresight, savings, or skills of the owners or managers of industry. The size of the labor force, its educational levels, increase in human knowledge, economies of scale made possible by the size of the country: who can make a rightful claim to having caused these changes, who engineered them, who controlled them?

Or consider the question of allocating the fruits of economic growth. Who ought to receive what shares? And how should the "decision" about shares be made? One answer is that shares in the growth in national income ought to be allocated according to individual or group contributions. If the contributions are traceable to social factors, however, and not to specific individuals or even to definite groups, how are we to make the allocations? How, for example, ought we to allocate the growth in national income resulting from increases in knowledge, in the magnitude and education of the labor force, in economies of scale? If the European Common Market provides greater economies of scale for European firms, to whom should the increases in the national income of the Common Market countries be allocated? Or take the broader question of an economic "surplus." Let us suppose (without making too much depend on it) that we think of a nation's economic surplus as a hypothetical sum consisting of what remains, if anything, after total national income is distributed in personal incomes sufficient for the subsistence of the population. Needless to say, "subsistence" is itself in large part socially defined. Whatever the prevailing social definition of "subsistence" and "surplus" may be, however, a country could allocate its surplus through different processes and in varying amounts for various purposes. Like the surplus itself, any "decision" about how to distribute it will be in some sense a social decision, for it is a complex of innumerable individual and collective choices, including many by enterprises and some by governments. To what purposes ought the surplus be put? Higher personal incomes? Renewing the existing stock of plant and equipment? Increasing and improving that stock? Improving the health or education of citizens? More leisure? And how much for each purpose? Few matters should be of greater public concern than answers to questions like these, few choices have greater consequence for so many people, few decisions made by governments are as important as the social decision about the distribution of the economic surplus—or, more broadly, the distribution of the national income.

Finally, consider a larger firm. A large firm is inherently a social and political enterprise. It is inherently *social* in the sense that its very existence and functioning depend on contributions made by joint actions, past and current, that cannot be attributed to specific persons: the arrow of causation is released by "social forces," history, culture, or other poorly defined agents. Without the protection of a dense network of laws enforced by public governments, the largest American corporation could not exist for a day. Without a labor force the firm would vanish. It would slowly languish if the labor force were not suitably educated. Who then provides for the education of its skilled workers, its white-collar employees, its executives? One of a firm's most critical resources is language. Language comes free, provided by "society" and millennia of evolution. Concepts, ideas, civic orientations like the famous Protestant ethic, the condition of science and technology: these are social. Who has made a larger contribution to the operation of General Electric—its chief executives or Albert Einstein or Michael Faraday or Isaac Newton?

A large firm is also inherently a *political* system because the government of the firm exercises great power, including coercive power. The government of a firm can have more impact on the lives of more people than the government of many a town, city, province, state. No one disputes today that the government of a city or a state ought to be a public, not a private matter. One who supports democratic ideas would also hold that people who are compelled to obey public governments ought to control those governments: no taxation without representation. Should this reasoning not apply also to the government of a large economic enterprise? If not, why not? (Dahl 1973).

If the economy and economic enterprises are social, if they are truly public entities, if like the government of a city, state, or nation their governments exercise great power, if they are political systems—then how ought these "public" institutions to be governed? If the economic surplus is socially defined and socially created, then by what means should it be allocated, and according to what principles of distribution?

It is unlikely that these questions can forever remain beyond political discussion in the United States. The ill fit between the perception of economic institutions as private, and their qualities as social and public, creates a discordance that probably cannot be indefinitely sustained.

Three Stages

While one can foresee how distributive issues might become more important in American political life, for reasons suggested in chapter 6 I doubt whether it is possible to prescribe a specific principle of distribution that can be shown to be superior to every alternative, much less to predict how much and in what ways Americans, after extensive political discussion of alternatives, would then choose to change the prevailing distribution of wealth and income. As I suggested in chapter 6, a number of reasonable distributive principles can be advanced; none looks to be clearly decisive against the rest, or still other possibilities; before any principle became binding it would have to be plunged into the heat and turbulence of the political cauldron; and what might finally be forged as a workable principle would probably be stronger politically but weaker philosophically than the abstract principles debated by moral and political philosophers.

It is possible, however, to foresee three stages of change. The first would be a change in civic orientations of the kind that I have just described. In the second stage, the United States would use employment, income maintenance, and tax policies to reduce economic inequality in the fashion already achieved in a number of other democratic countries. This would be a catch-up phase. In time, however, the second stage would run its course, because of electoral resistance, as it already seems to have done in the Scandinavian countries, and probably also because of increasingly disadvantageous tradeoffs with economic efficiencies, growth, and incentives. The third stage would require structural changes in the economic order that would simultaneously foster economic incentives, efficiency, and political equality. This stage has not been reached in any democratic country, though new proposals along these lines have begun to emerge. Meanwhile, the United States still stands before the threshold of the first stage.

Civic Orientations

Insofar as American civic consciousness is deformed by individual and group egoism, two possible solutions might be considered. We might hope (somehow) to foster greater civic virtue among Americans by strengthening commitments to the general good. Or we might strengthen enlightened egoism—what Tocqueville in his description of Americans called "self-interest rightly understood." Although the first seems nobler, it is less likely to succeed. In the last chapter I explained why neither moral nor organic civic virtue looks promising. I also suggested that the high coincidence of individual and collective interests required for individualist civic virtue is unlikely to exist among a large aggregate of persons, no matter what structural alternatives one might presume them to have adopted.

It might be thought that if individuals and organizations were sufficiently enlightened in pursuing their own interests, then they would perceive among themselves a perfect harmony of interests. Although the idea of an existing or attainable harmony of interests sufficient to rid us of our political conflicts is perennially attractive to some people, it is an illusion, and like many illusions it is a dangerous one. A common form of the illusion is to suppose that if Americans, say, were only to acquire a better understanding of the interests that in some sense "really" exist among them, they would develop a consensus as to their general good and the means to attain it; and, as a result, political conflict would dramatically diminish in intensity and frequency. The lethal defect in this view is that on some questions, "objective" conflicts of interest are sharp and real. The distribution of wealth and income is an example. Is it imaginable that a more equitable distribution of wealth and income could ever be achieved in the United States without intense political conflict?

While this illusion is more likely to be found among liberals and conservatives than among radicals, another form is more common among Marxists and radicals of left and right. This is the belief that some structural transformation would produce such profound harmony of interests that, following the appropriate changes in consciousness, the identity between individual and collective interests would be apparent to all and political conflicts would wither away. Socialists, for example, often appear to believe that replacing capitalism by social ownership and control of the economy would do the trick. But even if we were to adopt the unwarranted assumption that all serious political conflict is grounded in economic relationships, for reasons discussed in the last two chapters no unique answers can be found to a number of critical questions about the specific principles, structures, and processes required to achieve social ownership and control of the economy. How much autonomy should be granted, to which economic enterprises, on what kinds of decisions? How should enterprises be governed, both internally and externally? According to what distributive principles should the economic surplus be allocated? By what process of decision making?

After more than a century of dispute, socialists continue to disagree radically, insofar as they make any serious attempt to answer specific questions like these at all. It is therefore absurd to suppose that a single answer is likely to gain a general consensus. Conflicting proposals, rooted partly in conflicting conceptions of interests, would produce political conflicts. In addition, other cleavages—occupations, religion, language, ideology, local and regional attachments—would persist. And sometimes they would become entangled with economic questions; for example, how much of the economic surplus of advantaged regions should be transferred to disadvantaged regions? And so on.

One element of an enlightened civic consciousness in a democratic and pluralist system, then, would be a general acceptance of political conflict as an inevitable and entirely appropriate aspect of political life. An enlightened citizenry would understand that whenever the democratic process is applied to a large number of persons,

Type I solutions become impossible, and consequently only Type II solutions for large-scale systems are attainable.

A second element of an enlightened civic consciousness, however, would be a deep concern for ways of strengthening civic virtue by achieving a greater convergence of interests and a corresponding reduction of conflicts. Within the limits of Type II solutions and other limits I mentioned earlier, several changes would help to bring about a greater convergence of interests among American citizens. To begin with, the incentives of individuals, groups, and organizations to search for jointly beneficial solutions to public problems and their capacity to perceive their common interests and to cooperate in achieving them might all be made stronger. So stated, the proposal sounds purely anodynic. But it entails concrete consequences. If the interests of all citizens were perfectly harmonious on all public matters, political conflict would vanish and politics with it; but if the interests of all citizens on all public matters were strictly conflicting, a democratic order, and perhaps any political order, would be impossible. Although a perfect identity of interests is likely to remain a rare phenomenon among Americans, strictly conflicting, exclusive, and competitive interests—zero-sum conflicts— are also unlikely to predominate. The interests of different citizens involved in political conflicts are often neither perfectly harmonious nor strictly conflicting, but complementary. The interests of citizens would be perfectly complementary if, though not identical, the actions of each to achieve his or her ends would create benefits at no cost to the others. Perfect complementarity is no doubt rare. But interests are often imperfectly complementary, in the sense that for each actor the gains from cooperating with others outweigh the costs on balance. Conflicting interests make political life necessary; but complementary interests make it possible.

Citizens might come to perceive greater complementarity of interests, and therefore be more willing to cooperate, if they were more alike in their objective circumstances. A moment ago I suggested that it might be possible to reduce some of the great socioeconomic differences among citizens that result from extreme differences in wealth and income. Such a change, I suggested, is unlikely to be achieved without political conflict. However, some ways of bringing it about would probably cause less conflict than others. Meanwhile, the point to keep in mind is that as long as citizens are vastly unequal in the resources they have at their disposal, including their political resources, they are unlikely to perceive great similarity in their interests, nor do they have objective grounds for doing so. If "the general good" conflicts with one's own interests, one cannot realistically expect many citizens to act altruistically to sacrifice their own interests for the benefit of others, least of all those who perceive themselves to be significantly worse off than others.

In addition, certain integrative institutions might be strengthened, a question to which I now turn.

The Public Agenda

I suggested in chapter 4 that in comparison with a number of other democratic countries American political and economic institutions are less integrative and more fragmenting. That the political institutions should be weak in their capacity for integration is hardly surprising, since both the constitutional structure and extraconstitutional organizations like the political parties were shaped by a perspective that strongly emphasized the dangers of concentrating power and the necessity of allocating it to relatively independent centers. Although the Framers believed that by granting the states too much autonomy and the central government too little control the Articles of Confederation failed to provide adequately for national integration, they had no wish to cure the defects of the Articles by a too generous concentration of power in the new constitutional system. Political beliefs influenced by Hume, Montesquieu, and British constitutional doctrine (a doctrine swiftly outmoded by British practice) were reinforced by the evident political realities of the time, for even within the Constitutional Convention some delegates contended that the changes under consideration were dangerously centralizing, and a few left to join other anti-Federalists in opposition to the proposed Constitution. Consequently, in their search for solutions that would overcome the fragmentation of the Articles and yet avoid a concentration so great as to cause the Constitution to be rejected or, still worse, encourage tyranny if it were accepted, the Framers gave impetus to a stronger centripetal thrust in American political institutions than exists in a number of other democratic countries.

Four further consequences followed from the constitutional system, the political theory it reflected, and civic orientations that were to become widely diffused among Americans. The first, intended by the Framers, was to impede the operation of majority rule. In few other democratic countries are there so many obstacles in the way of government by electoral and legislative majorities. The second, unforeseen by the Framers but consistent with their intentions, was to ensure that when political parties developed, as they soon did, they would be more decentralized, more fragmented, less cohesive. And they would be less able to organize a majority coalition capable of uniting on and carrying out a set of policies than would the party systems that were later to develop in many other democratic countries, including a number of countries with multiparty systems. The third consequence, which was also unforeseen but contradicted the intentions of the Framers, was to make it relatively easy for pressure groups to influence decisions in behalf of objectives that are often narrow and highly particularistic. This consequence is not independent of the second. As E. E. Schattschneider pointed out several generations ago, the strength of parties in policy making tends to be inversely related to the strength of pressure groups, and in the United States the joint effect is a markedly weakened capacity for political integration (Schattschneider 1942, 192 and passim). Since the 1960s, fragmentation has been increased even further by the disintegration of the major parties into loose confederations of autonomous groups organized to advance the individual political fortunes of particular candidates—a development, as Schattschneider forecast, that has been paralleled by a rapid proliferation of narrow pressure groups.

The fourth consequence, like the third, was both unforeseen and clearly contrary to the intentions of the Framers: the development of the presidency into the main integrative force in the political system. From Jackson's time onward, the president has become the exclusive claimant to a mandate from a national majority and the only national official with some capability for forming and maintaining a majority coalition in both the electorate and Congress large and cohesive enough to carry out a program of reform against the resistance of well-entrenched minorities. The upshot, which the Framers failed to foresee, is an office of unstable and at times dangerous power. The antimajoritarianism of the constitutional system, the relative independence of president and Congress, the weakness of political parties, and the correlative strength of pressure groups have encouraged presidents to overcome the designed limits of the office by concentrating great political resources in the presidency and employing them in ways that are beyond the effective control of Congress, the courts, and the electorate. When reaction sets in against this excessive concentration of presidential power, the result is presidential ineffectiveness (Dahl 1977, 1980a).

Even without changing the Constitution, the political system does contain some potentialities for greater integration. The Budget Reform Act of 1974 provides an excellent example. Before that act was passed, budgetary decisions in Congress were a striking illustration of the irrationalities of an excessively fragmented process, for neither house of Congress had ever provided itself with an opportunity to consider either the sum total of expenditures that would result from piecemeal authorizations and appropriations or the relation between total expenditures and total revenues. A greater opportunity for irrationality in fiscal policy can hardly be imagined. In 1974, however, Congress transformed its fragmented system into a deliberately integrated budgetary process. Although fragmenting pressures persistently endanger the survival of that reform, it demonstrates that the constitutional framework by no means stands as a barrier to an increased integrative capacity.

The political parties provide another example. Their recent disintegration—the Democratic party in particular—is partly a result of reforms that were undertaken in a deliberate effort to "democratize" control over nominations and programs, though with an inadequate grasp of their disintegrative effects. Not only are these reforms reversible, but additional changes could further strengthen the integrative capacity of the party system: for example, more campaign funds could be channeled through the national committees, and campaign funding by the proliferating political action committees could be restricted. Moreover, if Americans ever had a mind to, they could, within constitutional limits, also transform their shambles of a two-party system into a multiparty system. Paradoxically, with four or five parties, each considerably more cohesive than either of the two loose confederacies, the process of forming legislative coalitions might be considerably more integrative than it is at present or has generally been in the past.

Yet the relative independence of president and Congress and the built-in conflict their independence creates cannot be remedied without a constitutional change far more fundamental than anything that Americans have until now been willing to consider. In designing the presidential office, and its relations to the electorate and the national legislature, the Framers had very little experience to go on; they found it exceptionally difficult to decide on a design, since every proposed solution seemed defective; and the particular design they finally settled on seems not to have been based on any profound rationale (Dahl 1981, 58ff.). Whether by accident or design, for the first century and a half the presidency, though occupied for the most part by men of stunning mediocrity, appeared to work satisfactorily. It no longer does. If the Framers were to assemble today, a vastly richer body of American and comparative experience would surely compel a different choice—probably something along the lines of the design they thrice adopted (a chief executive chosen by the national legislature) before turning finally to their solution of a president chosen independently by a college of electors (ibid., 66).

The weak integrative capacity of the political institutions is duplicated in American economic institutions. As we saw in chapter 4, economic organizations—businesses and unions in particular—are neither sufficiently inclusive nor sufficiently centralized to make a system of national bargaining either possible or desirable. Because the economic organizations are decentralized, negotiators would find it difficult and often impossible to bring about compliance with the terms of a national agreement; because the organizations are far from inclusive, in arriving at their agreements negotiators would have little incentive for taking into account the interests of the majority of people outside their organizations.

Great risks are entailed in a system of national bargaining by economic organizations that are both centralized enough to insure compliance with their agreements and inclusive enough to compel negotiators to consider the short- and long-run interests of a large and representative share of the population. But consider the alternatives: (1) Maintain the present system of decentralized bargaining by exclusive associations, which are strongly motivated to pass on the costs of their bargains to others not involved in the bargaining process and, like Congress before 1974, have neither incentive nor opportunity to consider the general and long-run consequences of their decisions. (2) Maintain decentralized bargaining but (somehow) make the organizations more inclusive, which would do nothing to increase the capacity for integrated decisions. (3) Eliminate the need for negotiation and bargaining by prohibiting all economic associations other than the individual firm, a policy that by requiring the prohibition of trade unions would be impossible to carry out today in any democratic country and, if it were possible, could be executed only at an excessive cost to fundamental rights. Or (4) Impose national economic policies without the consent of the economic organizations, and unions in particular, a task that has proved to be impossible in all democratic countries.

Alienation of Final Control

In the United States the extraordinarily successful adaptation of the ideology of agrarian democratic republicanism to the economic order of corporate capitalism that replaced it gave powerful support to the belief that, like farms, corporate enterprises should be privately owned and controlled by and in the interests of their owners. Yet when giant corporations make decisions that have enormous consequences for millions of persons who do not control those decisions, their legitimacy persists in uneasy tension with the democratic ideology to which most Americans also subscribe. On the landscape of a democratic country great corporations loom like mountain principalities ruled by princes whose decisions lie beyond reach of the democratic process.

It would be easy to diagnose the problem simply as an obvious conflict between democratic criteria and the private governments of corporate enterprises and to prescribe as the obvious solution democratic control over their governments. But the diagnosis risks ignoring the complexity of the problem and thus encourages simplistic and self-defeating solutions.

Alienation and Rights to Autonomy
As we saw in chapter 3, it is not always a simple matter to judge whether a people has alienated its rightful control over public matters. For the mere fact that an organization makes certain important decisions independently of the central government of the state is clearly not sufficient to establish alienation, even if the central government could not exercise control over those decisions, either constitutionally or de facto.

For we must first determine whether an organization's autonomy (with respect to some identifiable range of decisions and in relation to certain other actors or classes of actors) is derived from a fundamental right of its members. In chapter 3 I argued that whenever autonomy derives from a fundamental right of the members of an organization, it would be wrong to say that the demos and its representatives have irrecoverably lost, i.e., alienated, their final control over the public agenda; for they cannot alienate control over decisions they are not entitled to control. For example, if citizens possess a fundamental right to form and support political parties that can act independently in developing programs, nominating candidates, running campaigns, communicating with the public, and so on, then the fact that the government has no authority to deny to parties their autonomy on these matters can hardly be taken as evidence that the demos has alienated its control over public matters.

To be sure, determining fundamental rights in concrete instances is an exceedingly difficult problem, both substantively and procedurally (Dahl 1980b). But that problem is inherent in both democratic theory and practice, whether the theory be monistic or pluralistic, whether democratic institutions are on the small scale of the city-state or the large scale of representative government in a nation-state, and whether the constitutional system is unitary or federal. It would therefore be unreasonable to insist that to remedy the deficiencies of democratic pluralism one must first provide a unique solution to the problem of fundamental rights. One possible solution that has been adopted in a number of democratic countries is a system of legislation cum judicial review, under a written constitution that specifies certain fundamental rights. This is not, of course, the only solution, either theoretically or in practice, and not all democratic countries have adopted it. Yet in all democratic countries certain rights are held to be fundamental, in the sense that infringing them is considered impermissible, and processes exist for determining what these rights are and for ensuring their enforcement. Consequently, I shall assume that an acceptable process is available for determining fundamental rights and deciding whether an organization's claim to autonomy is derived from one or more fundamental rights.

Among the rights that might justify an organization's autonomy on certain matters, four are particularly relevant here. (1) Some political rights are necessary to the democratic process, in the sense that infringing on these rights would constitute an impairment of the democratic process itself. In chapter 2, I indicated what some of these are. (See also Dahl 1980b). (2) Arguably, in a large democratic order, citizens with common problems have a right to establish smaller democratic units for making decisions that essentially affect only themselves. (3) If freedom is a good, then freedom of choice may be in some sense a fundamental right. As everyone knows, to determine the zone of free choice that ought to be protected as a fundamental right is notoriously difficult and controversial: witness the question of abortion. I do not mean to confront the problem here. Yet it is important to recognize that whether we believe a claim to autonomy to be justified by freedom of choice as a value depends partly on where we mean to place the burden of proof. If we were to insist on a negative principle, autonomy would be denied to an organization except on a showing that the organization's autonomy is derived from a fundamental right or is justified on grounds of social utility. But under a positive principle, autonomy would be permitted to an organization except on a showing that the organization's autonomy (with respect to certain sets of decisions and in relation to certain other actors) is not, in this instance, a fundamental right *and* on balance is socially undesirable. The negative principle presupposes that autonomy tends to be undesirable; the positive principle, that it tends to be desirable. The negative principle reflects a bias toward centralizing control over decisions in the government of the state and against the decentralist thrust of organizational pluralism; the positive principle reflects a bias toward, not against, decentralization. Because of the intimate connection between freedom and political autonomy, the positive principle represents a commitment to freedom as both a value and a fundamental human right; whereas the negative principle implies that freedom is a danger and, at most, a privilege granted by a demos through the state. (4) Finally, a right to own property, and thus to use one's property as one chooses, might be understood to be a fundamental right, comparable to the other kinds just enumerated.

To the extent that the autonomy of various governmental, political, and economic organizations in the United States is derived from fundamental rights like these, final control over the public agenda has not been alienated.

Moreover, even when an organization's autonomy cannot be justified as a fundamental right, it might still be justified on grounds of general utility or efficiency. That is, the results of relatively independent decision making on certain matters by certain kinds of organizations are, on balance, beneficial to the collectivity. On these grounds it might be contended, for example, that business firms (whether privately or socially owned) ought to be relatively independent of one another and the government in their decisions about inputs, outputs, and prices, but subject to market controls. Conversely, if the results of an organization's independent decisions were on balance harmful to the collectivity—as decisions to dump chemical wastes in water supplies would be—then to prevent social harm an organization's autonomy could properly be restricted or done away with altogether. In a democratic order, judgments like these ought to be made by the relevant demos and its representatives, acting through democratic procedures and institutions. Indeed, conflicting judgments on such questions comprise a substantial part of political controversy in democratic countries.

Of course an organization might possess autonomy over some decisions as a matter of fundamental right, while its autonomy on other matters might be justified, if at all, only on grounds of social utility. For example, though citizens have a fundamental right to organize independent political parties for a variety of purposes and activities, the government of the state might properly regulate parties in order to protect the rights of members and to ensure that parties perform their functions effectively and efficiently.

Corporate Autonomy, Rights, and Utility
We can now see why in a democratic country the autonomy of private business firms is on a rather different footing from the autonomy of the other kinds of organizations mentioned in chapter 2, and particularly their nearest analogues, political, governmental, and

197

trade-union organizations. For the political rights necessary to the democratic process directly require a substantial measure of independence for organizations that facilitate the exercise of these rights, such as political parties, interest groups, lobbies, newspapers, magazines, and so on. A certain measure of independence over some range of matters for local elected governments might also be derived from a right of citizens to establish smaller democratic units for making decisions that essentially affect only themselves— though social interdependence considerably diminishes the zone of rightful local autonomy. Independent trade unions are more problematical; yet a strong case can be made that they are necessary both to democratic rights and to freedom of choice.

Obviously, it would be a very complex undertaking to survey the exact boundary between the zone of independence that organizations like these rightfully possess and activities that might be regulated by the government of the state, prohibited altogether, or transferred to government bureaucracies subject to control by the demos and its representatives. I think, however, that for a variety of political and governmental organizations, and probably certain "economic" associations like trade unions, such a boundary would secure a large area of autonomy derived from fundamental rights. To conclude that the government of the state could not control organizational activities within this privileged zone would not therefore establish that the demos had alienated final control over public matters to "private" decision makers.

But privately owned and controlled economic enterprises, particularly in the form of very large corporations, are a different story. For a large corporation is, as I said earlier, a political system, analogous in important ways to the government of the state. Yet the government of a large corporation differs radically from the government of the state in a democratic country, because neither in theory nor in practice are corporate governments democratic. Is the autonomy of large corporations justified, however, as necessary to fundamental rights?

1. It might be argued that by decentralizing decisions and political resources, an economic order of relatively independent firms gives support to the democratic process, and at any rate helps to prevent the concentration of power and resources that in the long run would probably undermine the institutions of polyarchy. The argument is, I believe, valid. But it is an argument for decentralization and not necessarily for decentralization to privately owned firms. In principle the argument would be met by decentralization to socially owned or employee-owned firms (Dahl 1971, 57ff.), either of which might in principle be democratically controlled.

2. It might also be argued that corporations are like local democratic governments, except that in the corporation the citizens are the stockholders. But "stockholder democracy" is a contradiction in terms, since it flagrantly violates the principle of equal voting. However, the claim might be justified if all those who were most directly affected by the decisions of a firm were, like citizens of a local government, ensured an equal vote in governing the firm or in voting for a representative government of the firm. But surely those most directly affected would include the employees; in that event, relative autonomy for firms owned socially or by employees and governed democratically might indeed be justified on grounds of fundamental rights.

3. It might be argued that economic decision making in a privately owned, competitive economy is reducible to private exchanges among individuals each of whom is free to agree or not agree to the exchange. This, the view of classical liberal theory, became an assumption of neoclassical economics. Under the positive principle of autonomy, it would seem to follow that every person is entitled to freedom of choice on any matter except where the exercise of free choice could be shown to be (a) socially harmful and (b) not a fundamental right. Although, as I have already said, making judgments of this kind is notoriously difficult, in my view this orientation is nonetheless a valid one. Yet while we might imagine an economy, as neoclassical economists did, in which all transactions

are reducible to voluntary exchanges among freely acting persons, when we descend from that imaginary realm to the actual world we realize how different the two are.

To begin with, as I pointed out in chapter 6, if the initial distribution of resources is unjust, then the outcome of the whole network of transactions that depend on that distribution is also unjust. In a democratic country, therefore, people might reasonably choose to remedy an unfair distribution of resources by using their government to redistribute resources, or to regulate particular transactions, or both. Moreover, because wealth, income, education, information, access to organizations, and many other resources are unequally distributed among different persons, in practice the persons who are actually involved in exchanges are not equally "free" to accept or reject a proposed exchange. To take a familiar and flagrant case, in nineteenth-century mill towns, children were not "free" to work or not to work in the mills—nor, for that matter, were their parents. Hence people in a democratic country might also reasonably use the government of the state to regulate or prohibit transactions marked by unequal bargaining power. Finally even among freely acting individuals, transactions may have harmful effects on others who are not parties to the transaction. These famous "externalities" so much discussed by economists also provide reasonable grounds for governmental control over the decisions of actors engaged in "private" exchanges.

If these and other discrepancies between our actual world and the imaginary world of free choice were to be removed, I have no doubt that the domain in which relatively autonomous "private" decision making would be justified as an exercise of free choice would greatly expand; and conversely, the proper domain of governmental control would shrink correspondingly. A fair distribution of income would itself significantly enlarge the domain of unregulated free choice. For innumerable choices that are now regulated in order to offset the consequences of an unfair distribution of income could no longer be justifiably regulated. Yet, as we know, the United States is

a long way from achieving—or collectively attempting to achieve—
a fair distribution of income. And even if we did manage to bring
about a fair distribution of income, many of the other discrepancies
between the real world and the heavenly universe of neoclassical
economics cannot be eliminated, particularly, perhaps, the externalities that are ineradicable in a highly interdependent society.

4. It seems to be widely believed in the United States that the
boards and managers of privately owned corporations do not actually make decisions on public matters because their control is derived from a fundamental right to property; and consequently they
are merely exercising their right to decide matters in the interests of
the owners. It is true, of course, that if the control of owners and
managers is derived from a fundamental right in property, then the
autonomy exercised by managers in behalf of owners of private enterprises would not constitute an alienation of public matters to private firms. For on this assumption what they do is a private affair.

Although this defense undoubtedly has great ideological strength,
it is badly flawed theoretically. For the justification of private property as a natural, inalienable, or fundamental right provides scant
justification for the existing ownership and control of large corporations. Insofar as a right to property is justified by the principle that
one is entitled to use the products of one's own labor as one chooses,
then surely the privileged position of stockholders is unjustified. On
this principle, indeed, the employees would have an even more fundamental claim to own and control the firms for which they labor.
Moreover, we saw earlier that economic production, growth, and a
surplus over survival requirements are attributable more to social
than to individual contributions and hardly at all to capital investment. Thus the principle would lead to the conclusion that the control and ownership of the economy rightfully belongs to "society." If
so, means must be found for "society" to exercise the control to
which it is entitled by virtue of its collective ownership. However,
the inalienable right of an individual to property might also be justified on the ground that a freedom to acquire some level of material

resources and to use them as one chooses is essential to many other freedoms (and hence a right to property is essential to the effective exercise of many other rights). Like the other, this principle fails to justify an exclusive claim to ownership of corporations by stockholders or other investors. Again, it would provide even stronger support to a claim to ownership by workers. Moreover, on this principle every person would be entitled to some minimal supply of whatever resources are necessary to "life, liberty and the pursuit of happiness." Yet to say that every one is entitled to a minimum does not imply that anyone is entitled to more than the minimum—and certainly not to an unlimited supply of resources.

Solutions

The anomaly will not go away. Many important decisions on public matters are neither on the public agenda nor decided by a democratic process. Consider two possible solutions.

1. For generations it evidently seemed altogether obvious to many socialists that the appropriate solution was to transfer ownership and control of economic enterprises directly to the central government of the state. In its limited version this solution means nationalizing certain key industries; as a general solution it means erecting a centrally directed economy. Considered abstractly—and for many years abstract speculation ran well ahead of experience—the solution seemed to many socialists the very perfection of the democratic process. Beginning with the demos and concluding with a specific administrative decision, the entire process was to be simply an extension of popular sovereignty. Within limits set by the preferences of the demos, or at least a majority, the representatives would make laws. Within the limits set by the legislature, the executive would make its decisions in turn. And so down through the chain of decision making through the industry chief right down to the last subordinate.

As everyone knows, however, bureaucracies are almost never mere agents of legislatures and executives. Officials in bureaucracies are motivated by concerns for their own power, status, income, security, popularity, policies, and ideology. Consequently, their goals rarely coincide fully with the laws and policies determined by their superiors. Because bureaucratic officials generally have access to enough resources for them to acquire considerable autonomy vis-à-vis their superiors, and strong incentives for doing so, they cannot usually be fully controlled by their superiors. As a solution for a small number of industries or firms, nationalization may secure a satisfactory measure of democratic control over bureaucratic decision making. But the more widely the bureaucratic solution is extended, the more difficult it will be for elected officials to control their nominal subordinates, and so the greater likelihood that the demos and its representatives will alienate their control over decisions on public matters to bureaucratic officials. Is a "public" bureaucracy independent of democratic controls any more desirable than a "private" bureaucracy independent of democratic controls? In one sense, both are private.

2. We return full circle to the conclusion at the beginning of this chapter that a limiting factor on all solutions is the need for some decentralization to relatively autonomous units in which decisions are regulated in part by markets and competition. Outside the unworldly realm of neoclassical theory, however, competition and markets will never regulate decisions so fully as to dissolve all economic activity into nothing more than fair exchanges among independent persons, exercising their full freedom to choose what is best for themselves and affecting only themselves. A satisfactory solution would therefore require at least two changes. First, the distribution of income would have to be fair. Second, decisions that would remain discretionary because of the inevitable looseness of regulation by the market would be subject to democratic control. But democratic control requires an appropriate demos. The solution of centralized bureaucratic administration of the economy was fatally flawed precisely because it implicitly assumed that the only appropriate demos for exercising final control over important eco-

nomic decisions was, in practice, the people of a country. But both fundamental rights and social utility provide adequate grounds for holding that different matters should often be subject to control by different bodies of citizens—just as they are by the governments of municipalities, states, and the nation. There is no good reason, then, why different kinds of economic organizations and different kinds of decisions made by the same organization could not be subject to democratic control by different citizen bodies; and as I have tried to show throughout this book, there is every reason why they should be.

In determining what discretionary decisions should properly be on the agenda of a particular demos, I do not see how the conclusion can reasonably be avoided that for those decisions which most affect their lives all the employees of an economic enterprise must be included in the demos. And to satisfy democratic criteria, citizens of a firm would have to possess equal votes.

I am aware that a solution along these lines is bound to encounter many objections and many genuine difficulties. Conceivably, an economic order fully under democratic controls would be unacceptably inefficient. But it is premature to adopt such a conclusion. Creative thought has only just begun its slow liberation from the intellectual hegemony of three misleading visions—the old monistic vision of a democracy untroubled by a multiplicity of relatively autonomous organizations and two competing visions of an economic order, one in which all the classical problems of ruling dissolve into voluntary transactions among free individuals, the other in which the economic order is democratized by means of the hierarchies of bureaucratic socialism. With these three great myths behind us, we may stand on the threshold of a period of creativity in searching for solutions to the problem of the economic order. There are signs that this may be so: the rapidly growing interest in possibilities for workers' participation or control; plans intended not only to redistribute ownership and control but also to strengthen incentives and increase funds for investment, like the Meidner plan in Sweden and the "wages fund" of the Danish Social Democratic party; American proposals for employee ownership; and many others. Ways of achieving an economic order that is both efficient and democratically controlled are yet to be fully explored.

I cannot say, of course, whether the changes in structures and in civic orientations necessary to remedy the defects in the American system of organizational pluralism will come about. To the extent that they do not, however, the United States will surely fail to achieve the best potentialities of pluralist democracy.

Appendix A

I have been puzzled by the assertion sometimes made by critics of "pluralist theory" that such a theory contends, or assumes, that all groups, interests, interest groups, and so on are equal or substantially equal in organizational capacities and access, or resources, or power, or influence, or the like. Thus Kenneth Newton writes: "Pluralist theory tends to work on the assumption that each and every interest is equally capable of organizing and defending itself" (Newton 1976, 228). But Newton does not cite a source to support this interpretation, and I have been unable to find other critics who do so. Since the proposition is on its face rather absurd, "pluralists" would appear to display an astonishing ignorance of ordinary social and political reality.

Although a careless reading of David Truman's *The Governmental Process*, which is frequently described as one example of "pluralist theory," might yield a proposition of this kind, Truman explicitly notes:

Several bodies of data, however, indicate: (1) that the frequency of membership in formal organizations of the association type increases from the lower to the upper reaches of the class structure, and (2) that the members of many, if not most, such groups are drawn from the same or closely similar status levels.

He then goes on to suggest that "the specialization of organized interest groups along class lines and the atrophy or deficiency of such groups in the less privileged classes may be a source of political instability" (522).

Who Governs? which is also often cited as an instance of "pluralist theory," opens with the following question:

In a political system where nearly every adult may vote but where knowledge, wealth, social position, access to officials, and other resources are unequally distributed, who actually governs? (Dahl 1961, 1).

A few pages later I provide evidence to show that

Running counter to this legal equality of citizens in the voting booth, however, is an unequal distribution of resources that can be used for influencing the choices of voters and, between elections, of officials (4).

It is possible that a regrettably imprecise sentence in *A Preface to Democratic Theory* might also be thought to support such a notion, though I do not see how that interpretation would be possible unless the sentence were lifted entirely out of context, as it frequently has been. The sentence is:

I defined the "normal" American political process as one in which there is a high probability that an active and legitimate group in the population can make itself heard effectively in the process of decision (Dahl 1956, 145).

Experience has shown me that even with the qualifiers the intent of the sentence is readily misunderstood, and I would write it more cautiously today. Yet the immediately following sentences are:

To be "heard" covers a wide range of activities, and I do not intend to define the word rigorously. Clearly, it does not mean that every group has equal control over the outcome.

In American politics, as in all other societies, control over decisions is unevenly distributed; neither individuals nor groups are political equals.

Among the possible responses to a group that is "heard effectively" I included "pressures for substantive policies, appointments, graft, respect, expression of the appropriate emotions, or the right combination of reciprocal noises" (145–46).

Nelson Polsby comments that "although pluralist 'assumptions' may start from something like the axiom Newton suggests, no pluralist research necessarily asserts the proposition as a finding of research or as a description of empirical reality." Moreover, Polsby would qualify Newton's statement even as a starting point for research: "Not 'each and every' but 'many'; not 'equally capable' but 'frequently in some manner or another capable, and depending upon the availability of a variety of resources, the skill and intensity with which they are employed, and the legitimacy of the group' would be closer to the mark" (Polsby 1980, 219).

Although it is possible that I have missed a source, the fact that critics do not cite a source and I have been unable to locate one strongly supports the conclusion that the proposition is not a part of "pluralist theory."

Appendix B

Although the weakness of socioeconomic class as a factor in American political life is well documented (e.g., Schlozman and Verba 1979, 103–38, 346ff.), on both sides of the Atlantic this weakness of class has long been regarded as evidence for American "exceptionalism." In recent years, however, a substantial body of accumulating evidence shows that, while rarely of negligible importance, in all democratic countries socioeconomic class accounts for only a small part of the variation in support for different parties. In addition to LaPalombara (1974, 424ff.), relevant comparative analyses include Alford (1967), Budge et al. (1977), Castles (1978, 103ff.), Haug (1967), Lehmbruch (1969), Lijphart (1977, 1979), Lorwin (1971), Lipset and Rokkan (1967), Nilson (1980), Merkl (1980), Rae and Taylor (1970), Rose (1974b), Nordlinger (1972), Pestoff (1977), Sartori (1976), and Verba et al. (1971). Relevant country studies include: Austria—Engelmann (1966), Powell (1970); Belgium—Lorwin (1966); Britain—Rose (1974a, 494–97); Italy—Barnes (1966, 1974), Sartori (1969); Netherlands—Daalder (1966, 1981), Lijphart (1975); Norway—Eckstein (1966), Rokkan (1966, 1967); Switzerland—Steiner (1974). Relevant country studies on Belgium, Germany, Italy, the Netherlands, Finland, Norway, Sweden, Australia, Britain, Canada, Ireland, and the United States are contained in Rose (1974a). In addition to the European countries described in Rose, Merkl (1980a) also provides studies of Austria, France, Spain and Portugal, and a comparative analysis of Sweden, Norway, and Denmark.

Works Cited

Alford, Robert R. 1967. Class voting in the Anglo-American political system. In Lipset and Rokkan 1967, pp. 67–94.

Arrow, Kenneth J. 1951. *Social choice and individual values*. New York: John Wiley and Sons.

Balbus, Isaac. 1971. The concept of interest in pluralist and Marxian analysis. *Politics and Society* 1:151–77.

Barnes, Samuel. 1966. Italy: oppositions on left, right and center. In Dahl 1966, pp. 303–31.

———. 1974. Italy: religion and class in electoral behavior. In Rose 1974b, pp. 171–226.

Barry, Brian. 1965. *Political argument*. London: Routledge and Kegan Paul.

Berlin, Isaiah. 1958. *Two concepts of liberty*. Oxford: Oxford Univ. Press.

Braybrooke, David, and Lindblom, Charles E. 1963. *A strategy of decision, policy evaluation as a social process*. New York: Free Press.

Brewer, Garry D. 1975. Analysis of complex systems: an experiment and its implications for policy making. In Todd R. LaPorte, *Organized social complexity, challenge to politics and policy*, pp. 175–219. Princeton: Princeton Univ. Press.

Budge, Ian; Crewe, Ivor; and Farlie, Dennis. 1976. *Party identification and beyond*. New York: John Wiley and Sons.

Cameron, David R. 1980. Economic inequality in the advanced capitalist societies: a comparative analysis. Prepared for delivery at the Harvard Univ. Center for European Studies and the Carnegie-Rochester Conference Series on Public Policy, 1979–80.

Castles, Francis G. 1978. *The social democratic image of society. A study of the achievements and origins of Scandinavian social democracy in comparative perspective*. London: Routledge and Kegan Paul.

Clark, John Bates. 1902. *The distribution of wealth: a theory of wages, interest and profits*. New York and London: Macmillan.

Connolly, W. E., ed. 1969. *The bias of pluralism*. New York: Atherton.

Daalder, Hans. 1966. The Netherlands: opposition in a segmented society. In Dahl 1966, pp. 188–236.

―――. 1981. Consociationalism, center and periphery in the Netherlands. In *Mobilization, center-periphery structures and nation building*. Oslo: Universitetsforlaget.

Dahl, Robert A. 1956. *A preface to democratic theory*. Chicago: Univ. of Chicago Press.

―――. 1961. *Who governs?* New Haven: Yale Univ. Press.

―――. 1966. *Political oppositions in Western democracies*. New Haven: Yale Univ. Press.

―――. 1971. *Polyarchy: participation and opposition*. New Haven: Yale Univ. Press.

―――. 1973. Governing the giant corporation. In Ralph Nader and Mark J. Green, eds., *Corporate power in America*, pp. 10–24. New York: Grossman.

―――. 1977. On removing certain impediments to democracy in the United States. *Political Science Quarterly* 92 (1977): 1–20.

―――. 1979. Procedural democracy. In Peter Laslett and James Fishkin, *Philosophy, politics and society*. 5th Series, pp. 97–133. New Haven: Yale Univ. Press.

―――. 1980a. Introduction to John Hersey, *Aspects of the presidency*, pp. ix–xix. New Haven: Ticknor and Fields.

―――. 1980b. The Moscow discourse: fundamental rights in a democratic order. *Government and Opposition* 15 (1980): 3–30.

―――. 1980c. Federalism and the democratic process. A paper prepared for the 26th Annual Meeting of the American Society for Political and Legal Philosophy, Boston, Mass., December 27–28, 1980.

―――. 1981. *Democracy in the United States*. 4th ed. Boston: Houghton Mifflin.

―――., and Lindblom, Charles E. 1953. *Politics, economics, and welfare*. New York: Harper and Bros.

Dahrendorf, Ralf. 1959. *Class and class conflict in industrial society*. Stanford: Stanford Univ. Press.

Denison, E. F. 1974. *Accounting for United States economic growth 1929–1969*. Washington: Brookings Institution.

Eckstein, Harry. 1966. *Division and cohesion in democracy: a study of Norway*. Princeton: Princeton Univ. Press.

Edelstein, J. David, and Warner, Malcolm. 1976. *Comparative union democracy: organization and opposition in British and American unions*. New York: John Wiley and Sons.

Engelmann, Frederick C. 1966. Austria: the pooling of opposition. In Dahl 1966, pp. 260–83.

Flathman, Richard E. 1973. *Concepts in social and political philosophy*. New York: Macmillan.

Frankena, William. 1955. Natural and inalienable rights. In Flathman 1973, pp. 450–56.

Goodwyn, Lawrence. 1976. *Democratic promise: the Populist moment in America*. New York: Oxford Univ. Press.

Hale, J. R. 1977. *Florence and the Medici: the pattern of control*. New York: Thames and Hudson.

Hart, H. L. A. 1955. Are there any natural rights? In Flathman 1973, pp. 440–50.

Haug, Marie. 1967. Social and cultural pluralism as a concept in social system analysis. *American Journal of Sociology* 73 (1967):294–304.

Haworth, Lawrence. 1973. Utility and rights. In Flathman 1973, pp. 468–84.

Hicks, John D. 1961. *The Populist revolt: a history of the Farmers' Alliance and the People's party*. Lincoln: Univ. of Nebraska Press.

Hofstadter, Richard. 1955. *The age of reform, from Bryan to FDR*. New York: Vintage Books.

Hyde, J. K. 1973. *Society and politics in medieval Italy; the evolution of the civil life, 1000–1350*. New York: St. Martin's Press.

Kariel, Henry. 1961. *The decline of American pluralism*. Stanford: Stanford Univ. Press.

Kinder, Donald R., and Kiewiet, D. Roderick. 1981. Sociotropic politics: the American case. *British Journal of Political Science*. (1981):129–161.

Kolakowski, Leszek. 1978. *Main currents of Marxism*. Vol. 1, *The Founders*. Oxford: Clarendon Press.

LaPalombara, Joseph. 1974. *Politics within nations*. Englewood Cliffs, N.J.: Prentice-Hall.

Lehmbruch, Gerhard. Sept. 1969. Segmented pluralism and political strategies in continental Europe: internal and external conditions of "concordant democracy." Turin: Round Table of International Political Science Assoc.

Lijphart, Arend. 1968. *The politics of accommodation: pluralism and democracy in the Netherlands*. Berkeley: Univ. of California Press.

———. 1975. *The politics of accommodation: pluralism and democracy in the Netherlands*. 2nd ed. revised. Berkeley: Univ. of California Press.

———. 1977. *Democracy in plural societies*. New Haven: Yale Univ. Press.

———. 1979. Religious vs. linguistic vs. class voting: the "crucial experiment" of comparing Belgium, Canada, South Africa, and Switzerland. *American Political Science Review* 73 (1979):442–58.

Lincoln, Abraham. 1861. First inaugural address. In Henry Steele Commager, ed., *Documents of American history*. Vol. 1, *to 1898*. 9th ed., 1973. Englewood Cliffs, N.J.: Prentice-Hall, pp. 385–88,

Lindblom, Charles E. 1965. *The intelligence of democracy: decision making through mutual adjustment*. New York: Free Press.

———. 1977. *Politics and markets; the world's political-economic systems*. New York: Basic Books.

———. 1979. *Policy-making*. 2nd ed. Englewood Cliffs, N.J.: Prentice-Hall.

Lipset, Seymour M., and Rokkan, Stein. 1967. Cleavage structures, party systems, and voter alignments. In *Party Systems and Voter Alignments*, Lipset and Rokkan, eds., pp. 1–64. New York: Free Press.

Lorwin, Val R. 1966. Belgium: religion, class, and language in national politics. In Dahl 1966, pp. 147–87.

———. Jan. 1971. Segmented pluralism: ideological cleavages and political cohesion in the smaller European democracies. *Comparative Politics* 3, no. 2, pp. 141–44.

Lowi, Theodore. 1969. *The end of liberalism*. New York: Norton.

Mackay, Alfred F. 1980. *Arrow's theorem: the paradox of social choice*. New Haven: Yale Univ. Press.

Martines, Lauro. 1979. *Power and imagination: city-states in Renaissance Italy*. New York: Knopf.

Marx, Karl. 1974a. The civil war in France. In Karl Marx, *Political Writings*. Vol. 3, *The First International and after*, pp. 187–236. New York: Vintage Books.

———. 1974b. Critique of the Gotha Program. In *ibid*., pp. 339–59.

McConnell, Grant. 1966. *Private power and American democracy*. New York: Knopf.

Merkl, Peter H., ed. 1980a. *Western European party systems*. New York: Free Press.
———. 1980b. The sociology of European parties—members, voters, and social groups. Ibid., pp. 614–667.
Mill, J. S. 1947. *On liberty and considerations on representative government*. Oxford: Basil Blackwell.
———. 1962. *Utilitarianism, on liberty, essay on Bentham*. New York: New American Library.
Newton, Kenneth. 1976. *Second city politics*. Oxford: Clarendon Press.
Nilson, Sten Sparre. 1980. Parties, cleavages, and the sharpness of conflict. In Merkl 1980a, pp. 205–234.
Nordlinger, Eric A. 1972. *Conflict regulation in divided societies*. Cambridge: Center for International Affairs, Harvard Univ.
Ollman, Bertell. 1976. *Alienation, man's conception of man in capitalist society*. 2nd ed. Cambridge: Cambridge Univ. Press.
Olson, Mancur, Jr. 1965. *The logic of collective action*. Cambridge: Harvard Univ. Press.
Pechman, Joseph A., and Okner, Benjamin A. 1974. *Who bears the tax burden?* Washington: Brookings Institution.
Pestoff, Victor Alexis. 1977. *Voluntary associations and Nordic party systems—a study of overlapping memberships and cross-pressures in Finland, Norway and Sweden*. Stockholm: Stockholm Univ.
Pocock, J. G. A. 1975. *The Machiavellian moment; Florentine political thought and the Atlantic republican tradition*. Princeton: Princeton Univ. Press.
Polanyi, Karl. 1944. *The great transformation*. New York: Rinehart and Co.
Pole, J. R. 1978. *The pursuit of equality in American history*. Berkeley: Univ. of California Press.
Pollack, Norman. 1962. *The Populist response to industrial America*. Cambridge: Harvard Univ. Press.
Polsby, Nelson W. 1980. *Community power and political theory: a further look at problems of evidence and inference*. 2nd ed. New Haven: Yale Univ. Press.
Powell, G. Bingham, Jr. 1970. *Social fragmentation and political hostility: an Austrian case study*. Stanford: Stanford Univ. Press.
Pullan, Brian. 1972. *A history of Early Renaissance Italy, from the mid-thirteenth to the mid-fifteenth century*. New York: St. Martin's Press.
Rae, Douglas W. 1979. A principle of simple justice. In Peter Laslett and

James Fishkin, eds., *Philosophy, politics and society.* 5th series, pp. 134–54. New Haven: Yale Univ. Press.

————., and Taylor, Michael. 1970. *The analysis of political cleavages.* New Haven: Yale Univ. Press.

Rae, Douglas et al. 1981. *Equalities.* Cambridge: Harvard Univ. Press.

Rawls, John. 1971. *A theory of justice.* Cambridge: Harvard Univ. Press.

Rokkan, Stein. 1962. The comparative study of political participation: notes toward a perspective on current research. In Austin Ranney, ed., *Essays on the behavioral study of politics,* pp. 47–90. Urbana: Univ. of Illinois Press.

————. 1966. Norway: numerical democracy and corporate pluralism. In Robert A. Dahl, *Political oppositions in Western democracies,* pp. 70–115. New Haven: Yale Univ. Press.

————. 1967. Geography, religion and social class: cross cutting cleavages in Norwegian politics. In Lipset and Rokkan 1967, pp. 367–444.

Rose, Richard. 1974a. *The problem of party government.* London: Macmillan.

————, ed. 1974b. *Electoral behavior: a comparative handbook.* New York: Free Press.

Rousseau, Jean Jacques. 1978. *On the social contract* (1762), *with Geneva manuscript* (1756) *and political economy* (1755), ed. Roger D. Masters, trans. Judith R. Masters. New York: St. Martin's Press.

Rusinow, Dennison. 1977. *The Yugoslav experiment 1948–1974.* Berkeley: Univ. of California Press.

Sánchez Vásquez, Adolfo. 1977. *The philosophy of praxis.* London: Merlin Press.

Sartori, Giovanni. 1969. European political parties: the case of polarized pluralism. In J. LaPalombara and Myron Weiner, eds., *Political parties and political development.* Princeton: Princeton Univ. Press.

————. 1976. *Parties and party systems, a framework for analysis,* vol. 1. Cambridge: Cambridge Univ. Press.

Scanlon, T. M. 1978. Rights, goals, and fairness. In S. Hampshire, ed., *Private and public morality,* 93–111. Cambridge: Cambridge Univ. Press.

Schattschneider, E. E. 1942. *Party government.* New York: Farrar and Rinehart.

Schlozman, Kay Lehman, and Verba, Sidney. 1979. *Injury to insult: unemployment, class and political response.* Cambridge: Harvard Univ. Press.

Schumacher, E. F. 1973. *Small is beautiful: economics as if people mattered*. New York: Harper and Row.

Schweikart, David. 1980. *Capitalism or workers' control? an ethical and economic appraisal*. New York: Praeger.

Shils, E. 1951. The study of the primary group. In Daniel Lerner and Harold D. Laswell, eds., *The policy sciences*, pp. 44–69. Stanford: Stanford Univ. Press.

Smith, James D.; Franklin, Stephen D.; and Wion, Douglas A. 1973. *The distribution of financial assets*. Washington: Urban Institute.

Staebler, Neil O. 1979. *The campaign finance revolution*. Los Angeles: Citizens Research Foundation.

Steiner, Jurg. 1974. *Amicable agreement versus majority rule: conflict resolution in Switzerland*. Rev. ed. Chapel Hill: Univ. of North Carolina Press.

Stepan, Alfred. 1978. *The state and society: Peru in comparative perspective*. Princeton: Princeton Univ. Press.

Sternberger, Dolf, and Vogel, Bernhard. 1969. *Die Wahle der Parlamente und anderer Staatsorgane*. Vol. 1, *Europa*. Berlin: Walter De Gruyter.

Stourzh, Gerald. 1970. *Alexander Hamilton and the idea of republican government*. Stanford: Stanford Univ. Press.

Thurow, Lester C. 1980. *The zero-sum society: distribution and the possibilities for economic change*. New York: Basic Books.

Tönnies, Ferdinand. 1957. *Community and society (Gemeinschaft und Gesellschaft)*. East Lansing: Michigan State Univ. Press.

Truman, David B. 1951. *The governmental process*. New York: Knopf.

Turner, Frank M. 1981. *The Greek heritage in Victorian Britain*. New Haven: Yale Univ. Press.

U.S. Census Bureau. 1980. *Statistical abstract of the United States*. Washington: Government Printing Office.

Vanek, Jaroslav. 1970. *The general theory of labor-managed market economies*. Ithaca: Cornell Univ. Press.

Verba, Sidney, and Ahmed, Bhatt. 1971. *Caste, race, and politics: A comparative study of India and the United States*. Beverly Hills: Sage Publications.

Wolfinger, Raymond E., and Rosenstone, Steven J. 1980. *Who votes?* New Haven: Yale Univ. Press.

Young, Roland. 1956. *Congressional politics in the Second World War*. New York: Columbia Univ. Press.

Index

Abortion: freedom-of-choice dilemma, 196

Abstract theory: implementation of, 63. *See also* Theoretical knowledge

Accommodation, 42, 154

Acton's aphorism on power, 104

Adams, John, 176

Affective bonds: of family, 27; boundaries of, 63, 147; conflict with capitalist theory, 153; undermine class solidarity, 158

Agenda, public: criteria for ideal democracy, 6, 47; final control of, 6, 50; distortion of, 45–47, 78; variety of control and domain, 79, 85; necessary inclusion of economic enterprises, 204

Agrarian democratic republicanism, 176–81

Agrarian myth, 178–81

Alienation: causes for, 47, 48; not from fundamental rights, 49; of control by demos and representatives, 203

Allocation: problems with, 183. *See also* Distribution

Altruism: need for redistribution, 119; and justice, 146; range of affective bonds, 147; in capitalism, 153; in socialism, 157

American Revolution, 161, 176

Anarchism: limits of, 3; doctrine of secession, 93; of economic liberalism, 109

Anti-Federalists: opposition to U.S. Constitution, 190

Argentina: government and ownership, 115

Aristotle: *polis*, 10; inculcation of virtue, 146

Articles of Confederation, 189

Arts, the: independence of, 27

Assembly of Athens, 9

Associations. *See* Organizations

Athens, Greece: limits on participation, 8; offices filled by lot, 9

Austria: destruction of polyarchy, 39; post–World War II patterns of conflict, 62; war-time government and ownership, 115

Authoritarian regimes: hidden dilemma, 3; suppression of conflict, 37, 62; defined, 38; liberalization, 40–42, 132; goals of internal critics, 41; democratization of, 81; self-management, 132

Authority: delegation of, 6, 47; humane mutual controls, 23; partition of, 65–66

Autonomy: dynamics of, 3, 16, 20–23 passim, 30, 52, 168; of different organizations, 19, 27–29, 35, 198, 203; determinism, 24; relative, 26; tendency toward, 33, 52; of subjects, 35; organizational rights, 50, 92, 195–97; consequences of, 90, 167; freedom of choice, 196

—economic, 28, 108, 112, 113, 198; first determinant for policy, 113; independence from capitalism and socialism, 114

219